E-books in Academic Libraries

D0851071

CHANDOS
INFORMATION PROFESSIONAL SERIES

Series Editor: Ruth Rikowski
(email: Rikowskigr@aol.com)

Chandos' new series of books are aimed at the busy information professional. They have been specially commissioned to provide the reader with an authoritative view of current thinking. They are designed to provide easy-to-read and (most importantly) practical coverage of topics that are of interest to librarians and other information professionals. If you would like a full listing of current and forthcoming titles, please visit our web site www.chandospublishing.com or email info@chandospublishing.com or telephone +44 (0) 1223 891358.

New authors: we are always pleased to receive ideas for new titles; if you would like to write a book for Chandos, please contact Dr Glyn Jones on email gjones@chandospublishing.com or telephone number +44 (0) 1993 848726.

Bulk orders: some organisations buy a number of copies of our books. If you are interested in doing this, we would be pleased to discuss a discount. Please email info@ chandospublishing.com or telephone +44 (0) 1223 891358.

E-books in Academic Libraries

Ksenija Minčić-Obradović

CP

CHANDOS
PUBLISHING

Oxford   Cambridge   New Delhi

Chandos Publishing
TBAC Business Centre
Avenue 4
Station Lane
Witney
Oxford OX28 4BN
UK
Tel: +44 (0) 1993 848726
Email: info@chandospublishing.com
www.chandospublishing.com

Chandos Publishing is an imprint of Woodhead Publishing Limited

Woodhead Publishing Limited
80 High Street
Sawston
Great Abington
Cambridge CB22 3HJ
UK
www.woodheadpublishing.com

First published in 2011

ISBN:
978 1 84334 586 2

British Library Cataloguing-in-Publication Data.
A catalogue record for this book is available from the British Library.

Typeset by RefineCatch Limited, Bungay, Suffolk.
Printed in the UK and USA.

To my family to whom I owe so much

Contents

Acknowledgements

There are many people to whom I am indebted for their help and encouragement in the researching and writing of this book. I gratefully acknowledge the support and good advice of my colleagues at the University of Auckland Library:

- Janet Copsey, the University Librarian.

- Chris Wilson, Associate University Librarian, Access Services.

- My colleagues who have shared their experiences of e-books with me, positive and negative, over the years; in particular Sonia Donoghue, Lynne Mitchell, Linzi Edwards, Nicole Mustatea and Neil Heinz.

I would also like to thank Lorraine Estelle, the CEO of JISC Collections, for providing me with valuable information and advice.

A huge thank you should also go to my partner John Laurie and my son Bogdan Obradović for all their understanding and help while I was writing this book. Special thanks should go to John for all the time he spent proofreading and improving my English. Without his patience, unselfishness and support I would not have been able to finish this book.

List of abbreviations

AACR2	Anglo-American Cataloguing Rules
ALPSP	Association of Learned and Professional Society Publishers
ARL	Association of Research Libraries
ASCII	American Standard Code for Information Interchange
CCSDS	Consultative Committee for Space Data Systems
CIBER	Centre for Information Behaviour and the Evaluation of Research
CISTI	Canada Institute for Scientific and Technical Information
CMS	Course Management System
DRM	Digital Rights Management
EDT	Electronic Dissertation and Thesis
EPD	Electronic Paper Displays
EPUB	Electronic Publication (e-book standard, by the International Digital Publishing Forum)
ERALL	Electronic Resources Academic Library Link
ERM	Electronic Resource Management
FRBR	Functional Requirements for Bibliographic Records
FTE	Full Time Equivalent
HTML	Hypertext Markup Language
IDC	International Data Corporation
IDPF	International Digital Publishing Forum

IFLA	International Federation of Library Associations
ILL	Interlibrary Loan
ILS	Integrated Library System
ISO	International Organisation for Standardisation
IT	Information Technology
JISC	Joint Information Systems Committee
MARC	Machine Readable Cataloguing
NISO	National Information Standards Organisation
OAIS	Open Archival Information System
OCLC	Online Computer Library Center
OCR	Optical Character Recognition
OLE	Open Library Environment
OPAC	Online Public Access Catalogue
PC	Personal Computer
PDA	Personal Digital Assistant
PDF	Portable Document Format
P-N Record	Provider-Neutral Record
RDA	Resource Description and Access
RTF	Rich Text Format
SGML	Standard Generalised Markup Language
SOAP	Simple Object Access Portal
TK3	Night Kitchen's Tool Kit 3
URL	Uniform Resource Locator
VLE	Virtual Learning Environment
XML	Extensible Markup Language

List of figures and tables

Figures

Tables

About the author

Ksenija Minčić-Obradović joined the University of Auckland Library in 2002 as Cataloguing Manager. She has worked in libraries in New Zealand and Serbia since 1983 in many different areas, including medieval manuscripts, early printed books, current serials and children's books. Throughout her library career, Ksenija has shown interest in developing library services and librarianship. She has published several books (in Serbian, with other authors) and many articles (in English and Serbian) in the area of librarianship.

Ksenija's current activities involve improving the usability of the library catalogue and using the latest IT developments to automate and manage cataloguing workflows and streamline cataloguing procedures. She is a registered member of the Library and Information Association of New Zealand (LIANZA) and has served twice as a convenor of the Cataloguing Special Interest Group Committee. As part of this committee, she actively contributed to organising cataloguing workshops and seminars.

She also has a strong interest in e-books. The University of Auckland Library, the largest tertiary library in New Zealand, has a world-class collection of electronic resources with the vast majority of these electronic resources having bibliographic records in the catalogue. Ksenija has written several papers and given a number of conference presentations and public lectures on this topic both in New Zealand and abroad.

The author may be contacted at:

k.obradovic@auckland.ac.nz

Introduction

Much has been written about e-books. They are a medium that puzzles and intrigues. Even my local paper has an article about them almost every week. Everyone has an opinion. They have been examined from many angles, by many authors, on many occasions. And yet, there are still more questions than answers in the field.

E-books have been both praised and criticised. Some commentators have predicted that e-books will completely replace print books; others have concluded that e-books are dying. Neither has happened – print and electronic books coexist, and in academic libraries both formats have a place, and complement each other.

In this book, I describe the situation as it is today, hoping that our experiences of the recent past will help libraries and publishers develop a better understanding of e-books, and how this powerful medium can best be used in the academic environment.

The book is based on my own experiences with e-book collections at the University of Auckland Library, as well as on the practices of academic and research libraries as described in the literature. Since e-books first appeared in libraries, hundreds of articles have been written about them, describing how they have been integrated into library collections and giving an excellent overview of the problems libraries have faced. I have been able to refer only to some of them in this book. Where articles have been published in subscription magazines as well as open source repositories I have generally cited the freely available version to allow all my readers to access it.

Many surveys have been conducted on e-books over the last decade. They give a good indication of trends in e-book publishing and e-book usage, and I often make reference to their findings. They have been done by both libraries and publishers, as both are interested in understanding trends in e-book usage.

Daily newspapers, print and electronic, and also forums and blogs such as the *MobileRead* forum, *TeleRead: Bring the E-Books Home* blog, and *The Digital Reader* blog, have provided me with excellent information on the latest developments. Many people, keen to test the latest e-book readers, are also happy to share their opinion about them, and they leave posts on blogs, or write longer articles on websites that follow the latest IT developments. They tell us how various e-readers compare in price, size, weight and features, and what their strong and weak points are. Some people even create video recordings of their experiences with e-book readers and post them on video-sharing websites, such as YouTube, allowing a more personal touch.

Companies involved in the e-book market also add valuable posts on their websites. For example, the United States-based company Aptara, which provides digital publishing solutions, closely follows developments in the e-book market.

Most of my own knowledge of e-books comes from my hands-on work with the University of Auckland Library's e-book collections, and I will often refer to these collections, to the problems that arose and the solutions we found for them.

I started working at the University of Auckland Library as Cataloguing Department manager about the same time as our first e-book collections were purchased. I soon encountered the common issues that accompany e-books. Ever since, together with my colleagues in technical services departments, I have been trying to figure out the easiest and most economic ways of providing access to e-books, and have been adjusting workflows to take account of the changes e-books have introduced. As our collections have grown, the situation has not become any less challenging.

The University of Auckland was established in 1883. It has over 39,000 students and 2,104 FTE[1] academic staff. It is both New Zealand's largest university and its top-ranked university based on research quality.[2] The University of Auckland Library is the most extensive Library system in New Zealand and ranks with the top five Australian university libraries. It has 227 FTE staff and serves over 50,000 users.[3] The Library has been eager to exploit opportunities offered by new technologies to expand services and support the University's learning and teaching initiatives. The University Librarian has taken a leading role in ensuring that e-book collections have featured in the Library's strategic plan. Today, the University of Auckland Library has a world-class collection of electronic resources, together with almost every challenge that accompanies them.

Access to the first e-books was provided in 1998, when the Library bought a new integrated library system (Voyager) which enabled linking from the Library catalogue to an e-resource. The first collection of e-books was bought at the beginning of 2001, and by the end of 2009 the Library had acquired over eighty e-book databases. The Library catalogue currently lists bibliographic records for nearly 350,000 e-books, but unfortunately, not all e-book collections have bibliographic records, and for this reason it is difficult to say what the total number of e-book titles is. E-books now represent almost 20 per cent of all material in the Library catalogue. Spending on e-books is increasing every year; in

2004, it was 3 per cent of a total collections budget of NZ$14,436,000, and in 2009, almost 11 per cent of a total collections budget of NZ$19,516,551.

Holdings of electronic and print monographs added to the Library catalogue since access to the first e-book was provided, are shown in Table 1.1. Figures for electronic and print books are not obtained in the same way, so they are not completely comparable. Figures for e-books are retrieved by a Voyager report, and they represent the number of e-books added to Library collections in a certain year that are still available, while figures for print books represent print books that were added to the collections in the same year, whether they are still available or not. Despite this, the figures clearly show trends in collection development over the past twelve years. In 2003 and 2004 the Library acquired almost twice as many e-books as print books. This was a result of publishers digitising back volumes and the Library acquiring some

| Table 1.1 | Print and e-book yearly additions to the University of Auckland Library catalogue |

Year	E-book titles	Print book titles
2009	30,161	45,225
2008	18,042	40,012
2007	14,321	46,868
2006	66,806	53,488
2005	40,746	50,340
2004	93,905	51,187
2003	81,890	46,757
2002	4,404	43,080
2001	5,261	43,467
2000	29	33,844
1999	3	29,340
1998	279	31,060

big collections, including *Early English Books Online* and *Eighteenth Century Collections Online*.

This book is written from the point of view of a practitioner, of a librarian who works with e-books literally every day. A significant part of my job is related to e-book metadata – adding new records, checking files sent by vendors and working with vendors and publishers on MARC records. As my job involves providing access to e-books, I also have to answer a steady stream of queries from subject librarians, such as: 'Why are there records for some collections in the Library catalogue and no records for others?' 'Why is this e-book, which has been used as recommended reading for the last two years, suddenly unavailable?' 'Are new books added to the collection as part of the entitlement or do they have to be bought separately?' 'Is there an easy way to know what titles are part of our e-book collections?' Often I was unable to give an answer, and, without even noticing it, I became one of that large group of people puzzled by the e-book phenomenon. I started reading about e-books, and searching for answers. This book is the result of those years of monitoring what is happening with e-books.

Several years ago one would often come across predictions that Internet access would make libraries obsolete. However, over the years, the scholarly e-book publishing industry has re-orientated itself towards libraries. Companies serving the academic e-book market have realised that the biggest consumers of scholarly e-book products and services are academic libraries, and they have focused their efforts in that direction. They have come up with a number of solutions specially designed for libraries. However, the extent to which they have been able to meet the needs of the library world remains a matter of debate. Many attractive platforms for libraries have been developed, but such a variety of platforms has been confusing for users, as well as for librarians. Further development in this area is very much dependent on both academic libraries and publishers and it is probably true to say that libraries have not managed to adequately explain their needs to publishers.

The impact of e-books on academic libraries is significant. The objective of this book is to present both its positive and negative sides and Chapter 2, in particular, focuses on this area. It discusses the opportunities e-books bring to academic libraries, outlines the features of e-books that are important in the academic context and pinpoints problems which have caused criticism. Chapter 2 also outlines the history of e-books, lists some definitions, and describes the various types of electronic monographs.

Chapter 3 reviews the current situation in e-book publishing and describes some of the purchase models vendors and publishers are offering. It discusses issues with free e-books (such as government publications) and their importance for academic libraries. It looks at the Google Books project, and other mass digitisation initiatives, and the effect these are having on the academic market. It looks at digital rights management in a broad sense, and its effect on libraries. The need for more digital texts is obvious, and universities are making their own unique and rare texts (such as theses and historical sources) available in digital format. This part of the e-book market is also described.

E-books promise to simplify library collection management, but managing e-book collections has presented many problems. The variety of purchase models that vendors offer, varying formats, the lack of standardisation, difficulties in selection and in obtaining bibliographic records, choosing avenues for access, and long-term preservation, are just some of the daunting challenges librarians face in integrating e-books into academic libraries. Chapter 4 addresses problems surrounding the management of e-books and gives examples of solutions.

E-books are expensive and academic libraries have to

ensure that they get value for money. Chapter 5 describes initiatives to publicise and promote e-books, such as user education programmes, dedicated e-book pages, and video clip demonstrations. It looks at library and publisher surveys of e-book usage, noting changes in user preferences and behaviour over the last decade. It also discusses usage statistics, how data is gathered, and how it can be used.

One of the aims of this book is to describe how e-books support libraries to align closely with the priorities of their universities. Chapter 6 discusses the changes new technologies have brought about in the academic environment. It describes e-learning initiatives, talks about the importance of electronic textbooks, and gives some examples of innovative e-books which have made good use of new functionalities.

The last chapter attempts to answer questions such as: What would make libraries buy more e-books? What would make library users use more e-books? How can publishers be persuaded to provide electronic textbooks? The book concludes with speculations on the future of e-books in academic libraries and identifies factors which will have an influence on that.

E-books have already changed the way libraries provide services, but there is still huge potential for further development. The book calls attention to the need for collaboration between faculty members, libraries and publishers.

Notes and references

1. Full Time Equivalent.
2. More about the University of Auckland can be found at *http://www.auckland.ac.nz/uoa/home/about/the-university*.
3. More about the University of Auckland Library can be found at *http://www.library.auckland.ac.nz*.

The (magical) world of e-books

Because of their dynamic nature, and constant development, e-books attract considerable interest but opinions on them are divided. They have been seen as a promising media, but also as technology that has failed to gain momentum.

Their potential in education and research was recognised early on, yet their adoption by academic libraries did not go as smoothly as the adoption of e-journals. Whereas electronic journals quickly became indispensable, e-books have appeared to lag behind.[1] Nevertheless, there is a belief that e-books have greater potential to change the information landscape than journals.[2]

Academic and research libraries have been considered to be early adopters of e-books. According to a survey done by the Association of Research Libraries (ARL) on 75 member libraries, the earliest purchases were in the 1990s with packages like *netLibrary*, but most libraries began acquiring e-book collections between 1999 and 2004.[3]

According to the literature, this reflects the situation in other non-members academic libraries. It is also important to mention that some libraries have been put off by the range of problems accompanying e-books, and they are still reluctant to purchase e-books.

The ARL survey further says that libraries listed 24/7 access, the opportunity to pilot new and innovative technology, and the access provided by consortial agreements as the main reasons for their original entry into the e-book market.[4]

There are, however, authors who say that e-book technology has been unable to overcome barriers of adoption. Nelson[5] and Wallis,[6] for example, point out that e-books have had difficulties crossing a chasm – the barrier new technologies must overcome before they become more widely accepted (Figure 2.1).

Yet, it is noticeable that academic libraries have been enthusiastic about e-books. University students are generally comfortable with digital content, and universities are inclined to be early adopters of new technology. As Nelson noticed, higher education has a prospect of bridging the adoption chasm on several digital content delivery technologies before other industries.[7]

According to the findings of the Joint Information Systems Committee (JISC) National E-Books Observatory Project, e-books have entered into the mainstream of academic life. As part of their research on e-books, JISC undertook several

Figure 2.1   Geoffrey Moore's Revisited Innovation Adoption Curve

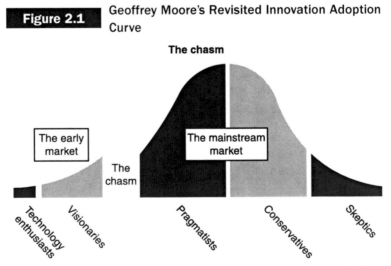

Source: http://www.exampler.com/testing-com/writings/reviews/page19.gif

surveys on e-book usage during 2008 and 2009. In 2009 nearly 65 per cent of the academic population of 127 higher education institutions in the UK were using e-books. The project has also shown that university libraries are important providers of e-books. One of the questions asked people how they got hold of their last e-book. Most respondents said that it was an e-book provided by their university library, with an increase in 2009 (52.2 per cent) compared to 2008 (45.4 per cent). The sources of e-books are shown in Figure 2.2.

E-book technology companies have developed a variety of solutions for libraries. Some of these solutions imitate the traditional library model. Adobe Content Server, for example, allows libraries to lend books to their patrons in Adobe PDF format on personal computers and handheld devices. Other solutions are opening new possibilities. *NetLibrary*, for instance, allows books that a library has purchased, as well as public domain books that *NetLibrary* carries, to be

| **Figure 2.2** | Sources of e-books (students and teachers) in the JISC survey |

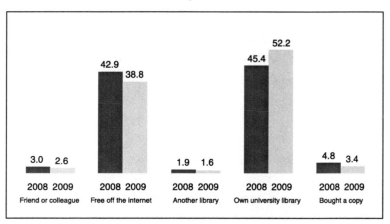

Source: JISC (2009). Headline findings from the user surveys: CIBER Final Report. Available from http://www.jiscebooksproject.org/reports/user-survey-findings (accessed 2 July 2010).

searched as a single full-text database. Features like video, multimedia and cross-referencing enrich the content and bring a whole new experience to traditional reading.

New technology has definitely altered the ways libraries provide services. However, administering large numbers of e-books is not easy. The variety of purchase models that vendors offer, varying formats of e-books, difficulties in obtaining bibliographic records, maintaining bibliographical control, and choosing avenues to provide access, are just some of the problems libraries have to overcome. Nevertheless, libraries that have already invested in e-books mostly continue to buy more, and to develop their e-book collections despite the problems they have experienced. The use of e-books in libraries is increasing and it is generally expected that this trend will continue.

Emergence of e-books

Many factors have influenced the development of e-books: the advent of desktop publishing; the growing importance of paperless publishing; the ease with which electronic information can be created, updated, copied, shared, distributed and searched; the availability of local and global computer-based communication networks; and the beginning of the electronic information explosion.[8]

The concept of the e-book has evolved over time. E-books have changed in format, content and standards, and the process continues.

In the 1960s, computers were used for 'computerised photocomposition or typesetting,' as it was then called.[9] The main purpose of computers was to expedite print publication. In the 1970s computers began to be used to disseminate information, and electronic publishing took on a new shape.

From that moment on, all aspects of publishing, from writing the text to final access by the reader, could be done electronically.[10]

The first e-books were mostly technical manuals and were intended to be read by small and devoted interest groups. But as early as 1971 Michael Hart had launched *Project Gutenberg*[11] with the vision of creating a digital library. Making digital books was a laborious and expensive task, and it took fifteen years for the project to reach the first 1,000 titles.

The 1980s and 1990s brought big changes. Some companies began to produce e-books on CD-ROMs and floppy discs. The arrival of the Internet opened major new business opportunities. In 1999 *netLibrary* was launched with more than 2,000 e-books commercially available to libraries. Other companies soon followed, including *ebrary, Librius, ZeroHour* and *Glassbook*, but almost immediately they ran into financial problems. The first websites selling e-books to individual members of the public, like *eReader.com* and *eReads.com*, were set up, and the first designated e-book readers were launched.

Wilf Lancaster, in his 1995 article *The evolution of electronic publishing*, recognised four phases in the 30-year-long evolution of electronic publishing: (1) use of computers to generate print-on-paper publications; (2) distribution of text in electronic form, where the electronic version is the exact equivalent of a paper version and may have been used to generate the paper version; (3) distribution in electronic form only, with the publication being little more than print on paper displayed electronically, with some 'value added' features; (4) generation of completely new publications that exploit the true capabilities of electronics.[12]

According to Judy Luther, e-books are the third wave of electronic publishing:

First, indexes from secondary publishers became searchable databases via online information systems such as Dialog in the 1970s and then on CD-ROMs in 1980s. Second, when the web became popular, primary journals began converting to PDF format for local printing or to the Standard Generalized Markup Language (SGML) format for enabling users to provide hot links to other references for further study.[13]

Terje Hillesund argues that the evolution of e-book technology is not accidental, but related to the penetrating impact of networks and information technology on society. According to him, economic and social forces created and shaped the e-book technology. He claims that e-books are a social necessity because e-book technology meets the requirements of the network society.[14]

What is an e-book?

But, before we go any further, it would be useful to define the term e-book. The terminology used for e-books is imprecise; they are often called e-books, or electronic books, but also digital books, and even online books. Even the spelling varies – e-book, ebook, e-Book, eBook.

Changing concepts of monographs reflect our understandings of e-books. S.S. Rao points out that 'the word e-book is often used simultaneously to describe content, format, reader software and reading devices'.[15]

In 2002, Armstrong, Edwards and Lonsdale defined the e-book as 'any piece of electronic text regardless of size or composition (a digital object), but excluding journal publications, made available electronically (or optically) for any device (handheld or desk-bound) that includes a screen'.[16]

The Joint Information Systems Committee (JISC) in their 2003 report define an e-book as 'an online version of printed books, accessed via the Internet'.[17] In 2007, Dinkelman and Stacy-Bates in their article, *Accessing e-books through academic library web sites*, repeat the Armstrong, Edwards and Lonsdale definition.[18]

In her 2005 article *E-books in academic libraries: an international overview*, Lucy Tedd notes that, according to both the *Oxford English Dictionary* and Wikipedia the term e-book is used ambiguously for the text and for the device. She also cites a definition quoted by TechWeb, a business technology network:

> Electronic books are handheld computerised devices with high-resolution screens, backlighting, and extended-life batteries intended to serve as storage devices for literary works or things like technical manuals that can be digitally distributed easily over the Internet.[19]

Since then, the definition has changed on Wikipedia and in August 2009, when I checked, it said that

> an e-book (short for electronic book, also written eBook or ebook) is an e-text that forms the digital media equivalent of a conventional printed book, often protected with a digital rights management system. E-books are usually read on personal computers or smart phones, or on dedicated hardware devices known as e-book readers or e-book devices. Many mobile phones can also be used to read e-books.

The current definition in the Oxford English dictionaries varies. The *Oxford Dictionary of English* (2nd edition revised) defines an e-book as an electronic version of a printed book which can be read on a personal computer or hand-held device designed specifically for this purpose.[20]

On the other hand, the *Oxford English Dictionary Online* has the following definition:

a hand-held electronic device on which the text of a book can be read. Also: a book whose text is available in an electronic format for reading on such a device or on a computer screen; (occas.) a book whose text is available only or primarily on the Internet.[21]

Crestani et al. in their article, *Appearance and functionality of electronic books*, see the e-book as a result of integrating classical book structure, the familiar concept of a book, with features that can be provided within an electronic environment.[22]

Sarah Ann Long says that 'e-book has become a convenient all-purpose term to describe a variety of reading experiences and methods for packaging and distributing digital content'.[23]

In this book, the term e-book is used to cover any monographic text made available electronically, regardless of size and composition.

Types of e-books

Modern e-books range from copies of print books to much more complex, database-type structures. They differ in the way they have been produced – some are digital reproductions of print resources, some are born-digital resources, and some are simultaneously issued in print and online editions. Although the heart of an e-book is still its content, it is important to distinguish between these types of e-books because they vary in many aspects, in their construction, functionality, price, and even in the type of readers they attract.

Digitised books and books issued in both electronic and print formats have less functionality than born-digital e-books. They may be full-text searchable, but by their nature they imitate their print counterparts, and they cannot have, for example, embedded audio or video like born-digital editions. Digitising old material brings additional issues. Typesetting was not standard in early books, and OCR is not easy. Additional work is needed to make them full-text searchable. Some collections, like *Early English Books Online*, include books as scanned images without any searchable text.

Price models too are very different. Authors of books in collections like *Eighteenth Century Books Online* or *Early English Books Online* are long dead, and there are no royalties to pay. The cost of these collections is usually a one-off capital cost. They are sold with perpetual usage licences rather than licences with annual subscriptions. The downside of this model is that once publishers have sold these collections to the worldwide academic market, they have little interest in improving the platform or functionality.

Born-digital books have living authors who require royalties and are likely to write new editions. Publishers struggle with pricing models in this context, and fear that their markets might be damaged. They are afraid that e-books will be downloaded and shared, and that students won't buy books if they are freely available in libraries.

Digitised collections differ from born-digital collections in the types of readers they attract and in the way they are used. Digitising heritage collections is of inestimable value but the reading public attracted by that type of book are generally small groups of students and researchers engaged in historical research. Born-digital books, on the other hand, serve all subject areas, are used by all type of readerships, and their usage is much higher.

E-books and their place in academic libraries

Modern universities encourage and promote the development of flexible educational models, the use of new teaching technologies and computer-assisted learning management systems. Flexible, distance and e-learning initiatives involve engaging students in online learning experiences. Together with other online resources, e-books offer excellent support for teaching and learning. Many university libraries around the world have been eager to find ways to incorporate them into the learning and teaching initiatives of their universities.

One area that is well recognised as benefiting from e-books is distance learning. Online education makes higher education more affordable and accessible, and the number of students enrolling for online education programmes is constantly increasing. Students can complete or advance their education while they work. Thanks to e-books, they can eliminate shipping costs, and reduce the number of library visits and associated travel time.

E-books have brought a whole new experience to monograph reading with the possibility of attaching video and sound files to the text. Multimedia capabilities have not been explored and used to their full potential as yet, but examples of their successful use are increasing. One example is the *netLibrary* audio file that pronounces words. This feature is popular in many electronic dictionaries. Multimedia can also be successfully used in education, especially in distance education when complex ideas need to be explained to students who are not present. E-books help learning outcomes in distance education match or surpass those in traditional classrooms.

Historical researchers benefit from being able to access digitised copies of old and rare books from their desktops. Collections such as *Early English Books Online* and *Eighteenth Century Collections Online* enable academics and students to access books which they would have had to travel the world to view in the past.

Universities are keen to facilitate digital access to scholarly works. They are digitising their own collections of theses and making them freely available on the Internet. Having theses in electronic format enhances their visibility, and encourages more use of them for further research.

E-books expand levels of library service too. The search capabilities they offer are extremely important for the work of library reference staff. The integration of full-text searching with other search capabilities allows librarians to search collections more comprehensively and mine considerably more information than ever before.

E-books have become an important part of the learning environment in tertiary institutions. Their importance continues to grow, and the number of academic libraries supporting digital collections grows with it.

E-book features in the academic context

E-books are often praised for their advantages over print books. E-book surveys show that some e-book functionalities are very important in the academic environment.

- *Access anytime, anywhere.* As instant access to information has become increasingly important, this is one of the most appealing characteristics of e-books. With ubiquitous and reliable Internet connection, e-books are easy to access at any time and from any place. This feature is particularly important for distance learners, but it is appreciated by all. Academics and students do not have to come to the library to check something; they can do it from their homes, or any other place, and they can do it at their own convenience. Academic staff are frequently away from their offices or travelling internationally and want to be able to access collections at times that suit them. Many students work part-time and need to be able to access library resources at times that suit their schedules. For them time is a very important factor, and finding resources online is a big help.

- *Saving of physical space.* Limited physical space is a problem for many university libraries. Library collections are growing and this creates a range of issues. Overcrowded shelves are more difficult to browse and books are more likely to be misplaced in re-shelving. Weeding is a time-consuming and laborious task. Physical space in libraries is very expensive,[24] and in this context electronic books are an excellent solution.

- *Full-text searches.* This functionality of electronic text is very much valued by users. Readers are able to scan and find relevant content much faster. Integration of full-text searching with other search capabilities allows more nuanced and comprehensive retrieval of information than ever before. E-book databases offer full text searches across the whole collection, not just one book. Studies on e-book usage show that the majority of users prefer print for extensive reading and use e-books for quick reference, which underlines the importance of this e-book feature.

- *Enriched text.* The digital environment has opened up possibilities for text to be enriched with other media.

Knovel, for example has 'titles with productivity tools', i.e. special interactive applets, such as tables with equation plotters, tables with graph plotters, unit converters, calculators, and graph digitisers that allow users to digitise curves by plotting points on a graph, and having them automatically displayed as the corresponding coordinates. E-books allow animated images and multimedia clips to be embedded. An example is described by Kurt Gramoll,[25] who explains how animations are used throughout a textbook to help present a case study or illustrate a certain concept. Gramoll argues that animated images are particularly useful in the discipline of engineering, where complex and abstract mathematical models and theories can be easily visualised through the use of appealing media such as animations, graphics, simulations and sounds.

Other functionalities of electronic text that are very useful include the ability to change font sizes and typefaces. This is particularly helpful for people with visual impairments. Text-to-speech software can convert e-books to audio books. E-books can allow non-permanent highlighting and annotation. Within the text, hyperlinks can be used for cross-referencing, and links can also be created to an external source.

Disadvantages of e-books

E-books are often criticised as well, and with good reason. Many of the problems that accompany e-books will be brought up in more detailed discussions later in the book. A few that have been considered the most important are listed below.

- *Reading devices.* E-books cannot be read without an electronic device and software – a PC, laptop, dedicated e-book reader, or mobile phone. Any reading device requires electric power. Users have to ensure that they are close to a source of electric power, or remember to charge their batteries. E-book reading devices are more fragile than paper books and more prone to physical damage. They can malfunction. E-books themselves can be damaged due to faults in hardware or software. If an e-book device is stolen, lost, or broken beyond repair, all e-books stored on the device may be lost. To avoid this, e-books have to be backed up, either on another device or by the e-book provider.

- *Variety of formats.* E-books are available in a wide range of formats: ASCII, PDF, RTF, TK3, EPUB and HTML, to mention just a few. This was one of earliest and most common complaints about e-books, but over time the situation has not got any better. Major software companies as well as independent and open-source programmers are continually developing new formats. Multiple formats cause multitudinous problems as not all e-books can be read on every reading device. Additional software may be required. This is confusing and off-putting for users.

- *Difficulties with reading on screen.* Computer screens and reading devices are improving, but many people still find it difficult to read on screen. That can be due to eye problems like glaucoma, but even people with normal vision find it tiring. Some surveys show that users find that it is hard to concentrate and absorb information when they read on screen.[26]

- *Compatibility with citation software.* Reference management software makes it easier to create bibliographies. It facilitates locating, managing and storing bibliographic references. Universities usually support a particular citation software package, and this may not be compatible with some e-book collections. For example, the *ACLS Humanities* collection of 2,200 scholarly books, compiled by the American Council of Learned Societies, is not compatible with EndNote, one of the most popular citation management programs. The *BIOSCIENCEnetBASE* collection is also incompatible with EndNote.

- *Technical requirements.* Printed books remain readable for centuries, but changing technologies and less durable electronic storage media require e-books to be regularly copied to new carriers. They equally require users to keep up with technologies, to have the latest versions of software and hardware. For example, one can use any recent web browser that supports cookies to access *MedicinesComplete*, but for full functionality the user will need a browser that also supports JavaScript. Some books available as e-books cannot be read on particular e-book readers because they are not supplied in a format those readers allow. As Landoni and Diaz noted in their article 'E-education: Design and Evaluation for Teaching and Learning':

> . . . development of e-books has been led primarily by technology instead of by users' requirements, and the gap between functionality and usability is sufficiently wide to justify the lack of success of the first generation of e-books.[27]

The above-mentioned article was published in 2003. In the meantime, much has happened in the world of e-books, but the gap between functionality and usability is still wide. The size of that gap and possibilities for closing it will be discussed in the following chapters.

Notes and references

1. Jenkins, A. (2008) 'What is inhibiting the proliferation of e-books in the academic library?' *Scroll*, 1(1).
2. Rowlands, I., Nicholas, D., Jamali, H.R. and Hutlington, P. (2007) 'What do faculty and students really think about e-books?' *Aslib Proceedings: New Information Perspectives*, 59(6), 489–511.
3. Anson, C. and Connell, R.R. (2009) *E-book Collections*. Washington, DC: Association of Research Libraries.
4. Ibid.
5. Nelson, M.R. (2006) *Digital Content Delivery Trends in Higher Education*, ECAR Bulletin, 2006(9). Retrieved 2 July 2010 from *http://net.educause.edu/ir/library/pdf/ERB0609.pdf*.
6. Wallis, R. (13 May 2009) 'Will the eBook make it across the chasm', *Panlibus Blog*. Retrieved 2 July 2010 from *http://blogs.talis.com/panlibus/archives/2009/05/will-the-ebook-make-it-across-the-chasm.php*.
7. Nelson, M.R. (2006) *Digital Content Delivery Trends in Higher Education*, ECAR Bulletin, 2006(9). Retrieved 2 July 2010 from *http://net.educause.edu/ir/library/pdf/ERB0609.pdf*.
8. Barker, P. (1999) 'Electronic libraries of the future', in A. Kent and J. G. Williams (eds), *Encyclopedia of Microcomputers*, Vol. 23, Supp. 2. New York: M. Dekker.
9. Meyers, B. (1996) 'Electronic publishing: A brief history and some current activities', *IP News* (Internet Edition), Fall. Retrieved 6 July 2010 from *http://www.lodestonesystems.com/doc/IPNews/pub/1996.4.EpubHistAndCurrent.html*.
10. Ibid.

11. See *http://www.gutenberg.org/wiki/Main_Page* (accessed 2 July 2010).

12. Lancaster, F.W. (1995) 'The evolution of electronic publishing – networked scholarly publishing', *Library Trends,* Spring. Retrieved 2 July 2010 from *http:// findarticles.com/p/articles/mi_m1387/is_n4_v43/ ai_17096178/?tag=content;col1.*

13. Luther, J. (1999) 'Panel at ALA discusses the reality of e-books', *Information Today,* 16(8), 38.

14. Hillesund, T. (2001) 'Will e-books change the world?', *First Monday,* 6(10). Retrieved 2 July 2010 from *http:// 131.193.153.231/www/issues/issue6_10/hillesund/.*

15. Rao, S.S. (2005) 'Electronic books: their integration into library and information centers', *The Electronic Library,* 23(1), 116–140.

16. Armstrong, C.J., Edwards, L. and Lonsdale, R. (2002) 'Virtually there? E-books in UK academic libraries', *Program: Electronic Library and Information Systems,* 36(4). Retrieved 6 July 2010 from *http://eprints.rclis. org/5987/.*

17. JISC (2003) *Promoting the Uptake of E-Books in Higher and Further Education: Joint Information Systems Committee Report.* Available from *http://www.jisc.ac.uk/ uploaded_documents/PromotingeBooksReportB.pdf* (accessed 2 July 2010).

18. Dinkelman, A. and Stacy-Bates, K. (2007) 'Accessing e-books through academic library web sites', *College and Research Libraries,* 68(1), 45–57.

19. Tedd, L. (2005) 'E-books in academic libraries: an international overview', *New Review of Academic Librarianship,* 11(1), 57–79.

20. *Oxford Dictionary of English* (2005) Oxford: Oxford University Press.

21. *Oxford English Dictionary Online* (2009) Oxford: Oxford University Press.

22. Crestani, F., Landoni, M. and Melucci, M. (2006) 'Appearance and functionality of electronic books', *International Journal on Digital Libraries*, 6(2).

23. Long, S.A. (2003) 'The case for e-books: an introduction', *New Library World*, 104(1/2).

24. Budd, J. (2005) *The Changing Academic Library: Operations, Culture, Environments.* Chicago: Association of College and Research Libraries.

25. Gramoll, K. (2007) *A Web-based Electronic Book (eBook) for Solid Mechanics.* Paper presented at the ASEE Annual Conference, Honolulu. Retrieved 6 July 2010 from *http://eml.ou.edu/paper/paper/2007_asee_fluid_ebook.pdf.*

26. Jamali, H.R., Nicholas, D. and Rowlands, I. (2008) 'Scholarly e-books: the views of 16,000 academics: results from the JISC national e-book observatory', *Aslib Proceedings*, 62(1), 33–47.

27. Landoni, M. and Diaz, P. (2003) 'E-education: design and evaluation for teaching and learning', *Journal of Digital Information*, 3(4).

3

Between publishers and library needs

The need for digital texts in academic libraries is growing as both students and academics increasingly appreciate their advantages. E-book publishers have become aware of this need, and started targeting academic libraries. Tertiary libraries are the biggest buyers of e-books, and publishers are developing new products to suit them. But to what extent do publishers fulfil library needs? Is the current variety of models satisfying or confusing for libraries and their users?

Librarians often argue that the e-book industry has been driven by the convenience of the publishers and that publishers have been conservative in moving into the e-book market and in their delivery options. On the other hand, publishers accuse librarians of not being proactive enough, and having too much of a 'wait and see' approach. Several speakers at the XXIX Annual Charleston Conference in 2009, a gathering of librarians, publishers and vendors, urged librarians to act 'quickly and strongly for positive change'.[1]

The complexity of e-books as a medium is noticeable on the publishing side as well. The following pages will describe some of the issues.

E-book publishing

Today's e-book market includes commercial and non-commercial publishers, as well as aggregators, companies that offer e-book content from different publishers. Libraries themselves are well into digitising parts of their print collections and becoming publishers too. Advances in hardware and software have led to an increase in self-publishing.

The majority of e-books in academic libraries are purchased collections, with much smaller numbers of free e-books and items digitised by libraries themselves. Each of these sources has its own idiosyncrasies, and each will be analysed separately.

Commercial e-publishing

E-books still represent a small proportion of total book sales, but they are the fastest-rising section of the market. Unfortunately, figures for e-book sales are elusive, as Vasileiou, Hartley and Rowley have rightly pointed out.[2] But even if available data provides only a partial picture, it is still a good indication of a growing market.

The International Digital Publishing Forum and the Association of American Publishers collect and publish quarterly data for United States trade retail e-book sales (Figure 3.1) on the Internet.[3] Their data represents the wholesale revenues of only about fifteen trade publishers, and does not include library, educational or professional electronic sales. Retail numbers are certainly much higher, and may be as much as double these figures because these are wholesale prices.

E-books are rapidly expanding their market in other countries too. According to Mark Nelson, sales are much

Figure 3.1   US trade wholesale electronic book sales

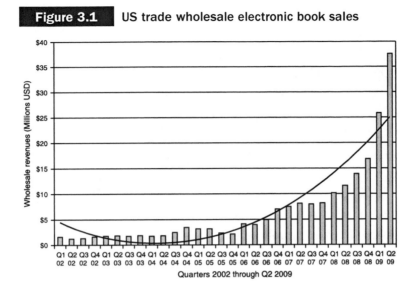

Quarters 2002 through Q2 2009

higher per capita outside the United States.[4] The situation in Asia exemplifies this.

eBook marketing report, published since 2003 by Impress R&D / Internet Media Research Institute, shows that the size of the e-book market in Japan has nearly doubled every year since the first survey.[5]

The Chinese eBook portal *du8.com*, together with the industry observer *China Book Business Report* publishes *The China eBook Market Development Report*. According to this report, e-book sales in 2008 grew to 226 million Yuan (US$33 million), which is a 33 per cent increase on 2007.[6] In 2009, sales went up to 300 million yuan (US$44 million) for legitimate, licensed e-books. E-book sales are expected to explode in 2010.[7]

The year 2010 was designated E-book year in Taiwan. The Ministry of Economic Affairs estimates that the revenue of the e-book industry will add NT$30 billion to the economy in the following two years.[8]

The number of publishers involved in the production of e-books is increasing and diverse and includes all kinds of publishers: trade publishers, smaller publishers, bigger publishers, university presses and scholarly publishers. In 2009, the Association of Learned and Professional Society Publishers (ALPSP) conducted a survey of scholarly book and e-book publishing practices. Out of 400 publishers, 171 answered the survey, of whom 63.2 per cent publish e-books, either on their own account or through an aggregator or e-book vendor. It is noticeable that the percentage of publishers putting out e-books increases with size – 80.5 per cent of commercial publishers publish e-books, compared to 57.7 per cent of not-for-profit publishers. Of further interest in this survey were publishers' attitudes to the Google Books settlement. At the time of the survey the settlement was still not ratified, and about 60 per cent of publishers had not opted in or out of it. When analysed by size, larger publishers were more likely to opt in than smaller publishers.[9]

A survey done by Apatara[10] included 300 United States publishers across the trade, professional and educational markets. The aim of survey was to examine future plans for publishing e-books and to find out whether e-books are important to publishers' business strategies. The survey found that over half of the publishers were offering titles in e-book format and that 65 per cent of publishers produce e-book versions of titles that are also offered in print. Sixty per cent of publishers who do not currently offer e-books plan to do so in the near future. Most publishers sell e-books through their own sites and produce e-books that cannot be read on most mobile devices, which means that publishers are missing the vast consumer audiences.[11]

There were new developments with the Google Books agreement close to the end of 2009. In 2005 the Authors Guild, the Association of American Publishers and some individual authors and publishers filed a class action lawsuit against Google Books. In October 2008 Google reached a settlement with book publishers and individual authors. The settlement presumed that Google will pay $125 million to settle two copyright suits over its book-scanning efforts. At the same time, Google will get the rights to make available millions of out-of-print books – including unclaimed works – for reading and purchasing online. Sixty-three per cent of the revenue from digital book sales and from advertising sold to accompany online user searches of the material would go to authors and publishers, and Google would keep the rest. Soon the settlement caused more concerns, and in April 2009 a formal inquiry was launched into the antitrust implications of the agreement.

The lawsuit was settled on 19 November 2009, and Google announced its intention to work closely with authors and publishers as industry partners, to bring even more of the world's books online, to the benefit of authors, publishers, researchers and readers alike.[12] Google has partnered with a number of prominent libraries around the world and with over 20,000 publishers and authors to make their books discoverable on Google. At the beginning of 2010, Google Book search interrogated the full text of over seven million books.

Google have also made known their plans for a number of changes. The agreement allows Google to make out-of-print books available for preview, reading and purchase. Readers will be able to buy full online access to millions of books. Libraries, universities and other organisations will be able to purchase institutional subscriptions. Google will also continue to point readers to libraries and bookstores where they can borrow or buy print copies. Because this agreement resolves a United States lawsuit, it affects only those users who access Google Book Search in the United States.

However, Google has expressed its hopes to work with international industry groups and individual rights holders around the world as well. Another Google initiative is to create an independent, not-for-profit Book Rights Registry to represent authors, publishers and other rights holders, which will help ensure that they receive the money their works earn under this agreement.

The Google initiatives to create a digital library of books are still causing a lot of criticism and many are sceptical of Google's data collection ambitions. In January 2010, the Open Book Alliance advanced a new objection on the basis that Google was using the settlement to fortify its supremacy in the search market and that it was improperly attempting to control the e-books market. At the hearing in February 2010 many authors expressed their opinion that Google's plan posed a threat to the authors' privacy. Competitors, such as Microsoft and Amazon, see the Google book settlement as an attempt by Google to set itself up as the all-powerful emperor of digital information.[13]

In an article published in the *Guardian* in February 2010, David Drummond, Google's Chief Legal officer, stated that somewhere in the region of 175 million books exist in the world today and that via Google Books users can access information contained in more than 10 million books.[14] As Mike McGrath noted, 'even Google is only attempting to digitise around 17 percent of all books!'[15]

The year 2009 also saw a positive turn in the e-book market. This was attributed to the development of wireless broadband networks and new advances in the technology of e-book readers, specifically reflective electronic paper displays (EPDs), and affordable, lightweight and portable e-book readers such as Amazon's Kindle and Sony's Reader, but also to developments in mobile phone technology, and smartphones, such as Apple's iPhone, having applications for reading e-books. The Horizon report says that 'electronic books have reached mainstream adoption in the customer sector'.[16] The year 2009 has been acclaimed as a watershed year in the evolution of the e-book market.[17]

Pushed by the popularity of Amazon's Kindle and the growing interest in digital books, manufacturers and developers are racing to meet consumer demands. The new Barnes & Noble e-book reader, the Nook, has a double screen and wi-fi, and enables users to lend books to each other as they might do with print books (although, this only applies to certain books, and depends on the publisher's wishes). At the beginning of 2010 Texas Instruments Incorporated unveiled an OMAP™ 3 processor-based e-book development platform which they expect to speed up the preparation of e-books for the market, and lower costs for e-book manufacturers and developers.[18] At the beginning of 2010 Apple launched the iPad tablet computer,[19] which can play music and video and surf the Internet but can also work as an e-book reader.

Only a few months after the launch, iPad had already brought some changes to the e-book market. Five of the six largest publishers in the USA (Macmillan, Simon & Schuster, Hachette, HarperCollins and Penguin) have reached deals with Apple to sell their books through iPad's iBookstore. The new pricing strategy is far more favourable for publishers and Apple's pricing model is already impacting Amazon, which has a 90 per cent share of the US e-book market.

Aptara predicts that Apple's iBooks will have a huge influence on the e-book market for four reasons:[20]

- iPad uses the free and open e-book format standard – EPUB.
- While E-Ink e-reading devices support only greyscale, iPad has a colour display.
- Implementation of Apple's own DRM to secure EPUB files will contribute to streamlining the e-book model. However,

this could also limit delivery and reading, thus undermining the publishing industry's effort to make e-books accessible across multiple e-readers.

■ iBookstore will bring changes in how publishers deal with all e-book sellers in the future.

Predictions of an imminent e-book revolution have been around for many years. However, the end of 2009 and beginning of 2010 have seen new developments and announcements on an almost daily basis. Is the long-awaited moment at last at hand, or is the excitement another letdown? At the moment it is not possible to give an unequivocal answer. In any case, it will be interesting to see the influence the latest developments will have on the e-book market, and particularly on scholarly e-book publishing.

Free e-books

The main publishers of free e-books are individual authors, government bodies, and libraries. There are also a number of special publically funded digitising projects.

The production of e-books does not require the use of paper or ink. The only requirement is software, and even that can be found for free. But even if software has to be purchased, this is only a one-off expense. After that initial cost, any number of e-books can be produced without incurring any additional expense. In traditional publishing, the price is influenced by the size of print runs. In electronic publishing that cost is eliminated. New or amended editions can be produced quickly at very little cost.

Savings in the publishing cost, as well as the speed with which they can provide publications to the public, are among the main incentives for government bodies to publish in electronic format. Some New Zealand government departments, for example, almost exclusively publish in electronic format. Their publications are key resources for many university courses and need to be incorporated in library collections. For example, the New Zealand Ministry of Health publishes reports on public health issues which are important for some courses at the universities, e.g. for population health studies. The Ministry of Education has a range of publications of interest to students and researchers in the area of education.

Other bodies also make their research freely available on their websites. Law Commissions, which are independent, government-funded organisations, review areas of law that need updating, reforming or developing, and make recommendations for legal changes or restructuring. Several countries, such as New Zealand,[21] the United Kingdom[22] and India,[23] have Law Commissions and they all make their reports freely available on their websites.

Many websites offer e-books that are out of copyright. Among the most popular are *Project Gutenberg, Internet Archive* and *Free-eBooks*.

Project Gutenberg[24] is the oldest digital library. It was founded in 1971 by Michael S. Hart. It offers nearly 30,000 books, available in a number of languages, and over 100,000 free books available through their partners and affiliates. Users can access e-books online, or download them in a number of formats, such as plain text, HTML, PDF, EPUB, MOBI and Plucker.

Internet Archive[25] is a digital library of Internet sites and other cultural artefacts in digital form. The Archive was founded in 1996 with the aim of providing permanent access to historical collections that exist in digital format. They have been scanning books and making them available for researchers, scholars, people with disabilities and the general public for free since 2005. Texts can be read only, or downloaded in a number of formats, including PDF, EPUB and DjVu. In April 2010, the Archive announced their two millionth digitised book, *Homiliary on Gospels from Easter to first Sunday of Advent,* a manuscript written in Latin on vellum in around 975 to 1000.

With an estimated 150,000 visitors per month, *Free-eBooks* proclaim that they are 'the internet's #1 online source for free ebook downloads, ebook resources and ebook authors.'[26] For ten years this website was a totally free download website but they are now offering two types of membership: standard membership, which is free for e-books in HTML format and limited to five downloads in PDF format per month; and VIP membership, which offers unlimited downloads in all formats in which *Free-eBooks* is offering e-books.

Apart from these three, the blog *E-books Online Free* lists some 180 websites with free e-books.[27]

Books offered freely online are rarely required and recommended texts for university courses. They are mostly recreational reading, but some of them may be supplementary reading, or material useful for research. But they have another value. Free e-books teach readers how to use e-books, and make them more familiar as a medium. Because of this, some libraries promote free collections. The University of Auckland Library, for example, has *Directory of Open Access E-books*[28] as one of the resources on its e-book portal page. Similarly, *OnlineCourses.org,* a portal to online courses offered by several United States universities, lists 22 sites with free e-books in its *100 Useful Links for eBook Lovers.*[29] *The Online Books Page* hosted by the University of Pennsylvania Libraries provides access to over 35,000 e-books that are freely available over the Internet.[30]

Libraries might also opt to provide access to sites that offer free classics, such as *Authorama*[31] and *Planet eBook*[32] or e-books that can support students doing foreign language courses, for example *Aozora Bunko*,[33] which facilitates free access to several thousand fiction and non-fiction books in Japanese.

Libraries as publishers

The demand for electronic texts is growing and many libraries around the world are producing digital texts themselves, becoming publishers in their own right. Among the reasons libraries go into digitising are to preserve rare and valuable collections, to make the research output of their universities more visible and to provide access to their unique material. The material they choose to digitise varies, and includes theses, unpublished research, and heritage collections of out-of-copyright books.

Several surveys have investigated the digitisation practices. Although they are not comprehensive and focus on particular issues from various perspectives, they still give a good indication of current developments.

A survey on digitisation efforts among 123 Association of Research Libraries (ARL) members was done in 2006. Out of 68 libraries that responded to the survey, 66 (97 per cent) reported having engaged in digitisation activities. As main reasons for digitising libraries cited improving access to the library's collection (100 per cent), support for research (85 per cent), preservation (71 per cent), support for classroom teaching (70 per cent), and support for distance learning (36 per cent). Material for digitising is selected mostly by collection development and special collections, and digitisation is done by preservation and special collections units, as well as in units designated specifically to support digital initiatives. Most libraries create metadata and in two-thirds of the respondent libraries metadata is created by cataloguing, metadata or technical services units. The most commonly used metadata standards are Dublin Core (92 per cent), MARC (84 per cent), and EAD (69 per cent). The most popular materials for digitisation are images and photographs, archival material, manuscripts, rare books and audio and video material. Fewer than half, but still a substantial number of libraries that responded to the survey digitise parts of monographs, complete issues of journals, and journal articles. Other material includes art works, photographs, maps, newspapers, 3D objects, slides, prints, and theses and dissertations.[34]

ebrary's Global eBook Survey was conducted in 2007 with responses from 552 individual libraries. Part of the survey was related to library practices relating to digitisation and delivery of their own content. The majority of libraries were already digitising their own content (32 per cent) or were considering digitising (24 per cent). The most popular items for digitising were special collections (63 per cent), images (48 per cent) and theses and dissertations (48 per cent). Most libraries (81 per cent) preferred to digitise their content in-house. Preferred formats were: PDF (78 per cent), JPEG (47 per cent), TIFF (33 per cent), HTML (33 per cent) and XML (27 per cent).[35]

The Primary Research Group conducted a survey on library use of e-books in 2008. Twenty-one per cent of the libraries in the sample had digitised out-of-copyright books in their collections and an additional 3.8 per cent planned to digitise some of their collections within the next two years. Interestingly, all the digitisers were tertiary libraries, and larger libraries were significantly more likely to digitise than were smaller libraries.[36]

The University of Nevada, Las Vegas Libraries administered another survey among ARL members in 2009. Results were received from 42 libraries and published together with the experiences of the University of Nevada Libraries, which are not an ARL member. The aim of this survey was to 'collect data on digital collections, understanding their respective administrative frameworks, and to gather feedback on both negative obstacles and positive inputs affecting their success'.

The survey found that more than half the libraries had digitisation activities as part of their strategic plans and that library administrations supported these activities. Making unique items available and themed preservation were highlighted as the most important factors when making decisions about new digitisation projects. ContentDM was the most popular platform for hosting digital collections. Many libraries supported several different platforms, while others had developed their own systems. Most libraries had an institutional repository on a different platform again. As the biggest challenges for their institutions' digitisation programmes libraries identified lack of staff, funding and support from technical staff, and lack of technical expertise.[37]

Heritage collections

Many projects are under way around the world to digitise heritage collections. General goals are to increase the availability to a world audience. Most of that material would be available only to local uses without digitisations. I'll mention just a few.

Early New Zealand Books Online[38] is a collection provided by the University of Auckland Library. The collection comprises books about New Zealand published between 1800 and 1870, and covering traditional Maori society and culture and early British settlement in New Zealand. The database contains full text and can be searched by keyword. Texts are proofread and an index of variant spellings has been compiled. The collection is still growing and at the end of 2009, around 240 texts were available. This is an in-house project that uses FineReader 9 OCR software to produce TEI-compliant XML files. B-engine software converts these on the fly to HTML files, and lately to PDF files too, for web display and links text to images of the original pages. Details of design parameters for the database and the technical processes used to convert printed text and images to electronic format for presentation on the web were explained by John Laurie at the VALA 2006 conference.[39]

The Wright American Fiction[40] collection brings together nineteenth-century American fiction, based on Lyle Wright's bibliographical work titled *American Fiction, 1851–1875*, published in 1957 and revised in 1965. The collection contains over 2,800 volumes and aims to include every novel published in the United States from 1851 to 1875. It includes works by well-known writers such as Louisa May Alcott, Mark Twain, Nathaniel Hawthorne, Herman Melville and Harriet Beecher Stowe, along with a great many forgotten authors.

This project, undertaken by nine US libraries (Indiana University, Michigan State University, Ohio State University, University of Illinois – Chicago, University of Illinois – Urbana-Champaign, University of Iowa, University of Michigan, University of Minnesota and University of Wisconsin) is not yet complete. The collection currently comprises two rather different groups of texts. The larger is a group of electronic texts created by Optical Character Recognition (OCR) software. These texts are available for searching and browsing, using the digital page images. The text files have not been proofread or corrected, and still contain errors. A second group of fully edited texts offers a corrected electronic text as well as the page images.

HathiTrust is a collaborative effort of major research libraries in the United States to archive and share their digitised collections. It was started by the thirteen universities of the Committee on Institutional Cooperation, the University of California system, and the University of Virginia to establish a repository for those universities. The *HathiTrust* collection currently contains over five million volumes, of which 750,000 are in the public domain.[41]

The Universal Digital Library, or the Million Book Collection, is a project initiated by the Carnegie Mellon University. The goal of the project is to digitise the published works of humankind and make them freely available online. Working with government and research partners in India and China, the project involves scanning books in many languages, using OCR to enable full text searching, and providing free-to-read access to the books on the web. By the end of 2007 they had completed the scanning of 1.5 million books and had made the entire database publicly accessible.[42]

Almost every national library has an ongoing project to digitise their national heritage. *The European Library*[43] is a portal that offers access to material from 47 European national libraries. It delivers metadata records as well as digital objects; some free, some at a cost.

Also worth mentioning is the *World Digital Library*, a collaborative project of the US Library of Congress, UNESCO and partners throughout the world. It includes important and culturally significant content from every UNESCO member country, including manuscripts, maps, rare books, recordings, films, prints and photographs.[44]

Digital repositories

A key part of the academic research process is publishing results. Open access is seen by many as a way to increase the reach and speed of scholarly communication. Both principles are represented in the institutional repository which is an archive of the scholarly output of an institution. They provide an opportunity for staff to publish their research electronically. Clifford Lynch calls them an 'essential infrastructure for scholarship in the digital age'.[45]

Gary Hall argues that all academic research and scholarship should be made available in online open-access archives.[46] As research is publicly funded, open access is something that can maximise social returns on public investments.

A report titled *The Open Access Citation Advantage: Studies and Results To Date* was published in February 2010 and examined 33 individual studies on the relationship between open access and citation frequency numbers. The report shows that increased visibility and accessibility for research articles, increases citations made to those articles.[47]

The developers of DSpace, an open source software commonly used as the base platform for institutional repositories, have pointed out that 'running such an institutionally-based, multidisciplinary repository is increasingly seen as a natural role for the libraries and archives of research and teaching organizations'.[48]

Repositories enable easy management of research material and scholarly publications, but populating an institutional repository is not a straightforward task. Usually staff members have little knowledge and little motivation to use it. Talking about Cornell University experiences, Davis and Connolly list a number of reasons why staff do not use repositories, including redundancy of other modes of disseminating information, the learning curve, confusion about copyright, fear of plagiarism and having one's work scooped, associating one's work with items of inconsistent quality, and concerns about whether posting a manuscript constitutes 'publishing'.[49]

Nevertheless, there are many examples of successful repositories. Well-known and widely used examples of institution-specific repositories are MIT[50] and the University of California.[51] There are also examples of discipline-specific repositories, like the Cornell University Library's *arXiv.org*, and examples of collaborative projects such as *Repositories Aotearoa*.[52]

Digital repositories capture a range of material: working papers, conference papers, pre-and post-print journal articles, teaching materials, datasets, and other forms of scholarship that don't usually see formal publication. Possibly their biggest value currently is their provision of digital theses.

There are also examples of e-books in repositories, such as the *Research in Anthropology and Linguistics* series, published by the Department of Anthropology of the University of Auckland, New Zealand. The series is no longer published in hard copy, and electronic copies are stored in ResearchSpace, the University of Auckland Library digital repository.[53] Since the series appeared in the repository, the department has received numerous comments from colleagues around the world, from people who would never have seen copies of the print editions. This is an obvious confirmation that electronic repository-based availability has increased the visibility of this series.

Electronic dissertations and theses

One of the earliest Electronic Dissertation and Thesis (EDT) initiatives was the National Digital Library of Theses and Dissertations (NDLTD) led by Virginia Tech, Blacksburg, Virginia.[54] Since its setting up in 1996, over a hundred universities have joined. Nowadays NDLTD is an international organisation dedicated to promoting the adoption, creation, use, dissemination and preservation of electronic analogues to traditional paper-based theses and dissertations.[55]

The visibility and accessibility of the postgraduate research output of universities is improved by EDTs. All universities that have monitored usage of their theses collection report that EDTs are used at least several times more than paper counterparts. EDTs also enable libraries to play a more prominent role in supporting research in their universities. The practice of making digital versions of theses and dissertations available on the Internet is becoming common in universities all over the world.

Setting up an electronic thesis and dissertation repository requires a number of alterations to existing copyright agreements between authors and the institution.[56] It also raises the question of how to store and manage the collections.

Libraries have different approaches to organising EDT repositories. Some, like the University of Auckland Library, maintain their own repository. In contrast, the Australian Digital Theses Program,[57] originally developed by seven Australian universities, now has 42 members from both Australian and New Zealand universities.

In the United Kingdom, the Joint Information Systems Committee (JISC) has funded research to create and test a national infrastructure for the storage, management and provision of e-theses. The project has provided the higher education community with guidelines on establishing their own institutional e-theses collections.[58] The British Library hosts the interface for the EThOS database of over 250,000 dissertations and theses.[59] The aim of EThOS is to offer a single point of access for all theses produced by UK higher education institutions.

Integration of e-books

The number of universities that support subscription to e-book collections is increasing. Not all have implemented e-books to the same extent, and their approaches have been diverse. Many articles describe the incorporation of e-books in academic libraries around the world. Libraries have followed different routes in implementation and found various solutions, but all agree that managing e-book collections is a challenging task.

Some libraries did pre-implementation research to evaluate e-books, and developed operating guidelines. The University of California's California Digital Library formed an e-book task force in 2000 to define operating guidelines and desirable features that will make e-books most useful for instruction and research in the University of California.[60]

Realising that introducing e-books to libraries requires significant planning and resources, Springer, a leading scholarly e-book publisher, has prepared a list of ten best practices for implementing an e-book strategy:[61]

1. Determine collection development strategy.
2. Evaluate different business models.
3. Gain internal support.
4. Plan policy changes with subject specialists/librarian liaisons.
5. Discuss implementation with technical staff.
6. Choose collections and vendors.
7. Link e-books to the OPAC.
8. Communicate to users.
9. Download usage statistics.
10. Review/renew.

Price of e-books and purchase models

Academic libraries have to set aside a proportion of their budget for e-books, and price is an important consideration.

General opinion is that cost reductions are achieved in e-book production by a book not being printed, and lower prices compared to print books is often mentioned as an advantage of e-books. The cost of print books includes paper, ink, trucks, gasoline, storage, shipping, shelf space, and the people involved in all these transactions. E-book production costs are much lower, and they do not get shipped in the traditional sense. However, retail prices of e-books and print books are very similar, and e-books are often more expensive than print books.

According to Ron Boehm, Chairman and CEO of ABC-CLIO Publishing, the cost of not printing a book is actually quite small. In his text *The Economics of Publishing and eBooks*, published on the blog *No Shelf Required*, he says:

> So, if the price of a book were set entirely by costs (which I'll argue is a very poor way of setting prices) the price of the book could go down by only $2.50 BEFORE adding incremental costs which ARP [All-Reference Press] incurs to sell the e-book. (Those of you who are good with numbers may realize that the list price could actually go down approximately $3.25. The net amount for the publisher would then go down $2.50.)[62]

He also says that there are additional costs in making e-books available:

> At the very least, if ARP uses only e-book distributors and does not host its own books, there will be some extra production costs to prepare the files into the appropriate formats, and staff time to transfer files and metadata to the e-book host(s). For simplicity, let's assume these are costs which roughly offset the $2.50 cent per unit printing cost reduction. [63]

Readers, on the other hand, expect the price of e-books to be lower than print books. It is interesting to note the protest by Amazon Kindle owners who were using Amazon's own book-tagging system to mark e-books priced at more than $10 with the tag '$9.99 boycott'. Their argument was that a Kindle book was more restricted in its use than a paper book and therefore should not cost as much.[64]

According to *ebrary's Global eBook Survey*, price is the most important thing libraries look for when purchasing electronic titles (Figure 3.2) or subscribing to an electronic database (Figure 3.3), just above the subject, access models and currency of collection.[65]

In a 2007 Springer survey on e-book adoption and usage, librarians were asked to rate the significance of individual cost items. The survey has shown that e-books 'provided clear advantages over print publications in costs associated with physical handling, processing and storage'[66] (Figure 3.4).

E-book vendors and publishers offer e-book collections via diverse platforms and purchasing models.

■ **Aggregator databases.** Following the serial model, most e-books are marketed as packaged collections. Collections

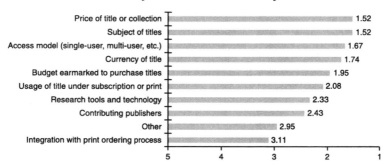

Figure 3.2 The most important things libraries look for when purchasing electronic titles (1= most important and 5 = least important) according to *ebrary's Global eBook Survey*

Price of title or collection	1.52
Subject of titles	1.52
Access model (single-user, multi-user, etc.)	1.67
Currency of title	1.74
Budget earmarked to purchase titles	1.95
Usage of title under subscription or print	2.08
Research tools and technology	2.33
Contributing publishers	2.43
Other	2.95
Integration with print ordering process	3.11

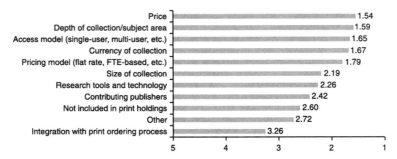

Figure 3.3 The most important things libraries look for when subscribing to an electronic database (1= most important and 5 = least important) according to *ebrary's Global eBook Survey*

Price	1.54
Depth of collection/subject area	1.59
Access model (single-user, multi-user, etc.)	1.65
Currency of collection	1.67
Pricing model (flat rate, FTE-based, etc.)	1.79
Size of collection	2.19
Research tools and technology	2.26
Contributing publishers	2.42
Not included in print holdings	2.60
Other	2.72
Integration with print ordering process	3.26

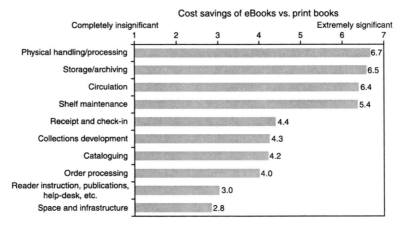

Figure 3.4 Significance of individual cost items in the 2007 Springer survey

Cost savings of eBooks vs. print books

Completely insignificant 1 — Extremely significant 7

Physical handling/processing	6.7
Storage/archiving	6.5
Circulation	6.4
Shelf maintenance	5.4
Receipt and check-in	4.4
Collections development	4.3
Cataloguing	4.2
Order processing	4.0
Reader instruction, publications, help-desk, etc.	3.0
Space and infrastructure	2.8

offered via this model include *ebrary, Knovel,* and *Gale Virtual Reference Library.* The advantage of buying e-books through aggregators is that very little time is spent on selection. The downside is that libraries end up with material that is of little or no interest to them, and that may never be used.

- Some databases follow a print books model. *NetLibrary,* for example, offers **title by title selection.** This model gives librarians more control over selection of the material, but it is more time-consuming than buying a whole collection. Nevertheless, some libraries are very keen to retain control over selection, and some vendors traditionally known as database vendors, have started to offer the purchase of individual titles as an option. This is the case with *ebrary*.

NetLibrary follows the print model even further and offers single-user access. This means that only one user at a time can view the content of an e-book, and once checked out, it cannot be accessed by another user until it is checked in again. This approach was criticised by many libraries, and as a result some changes have been introduced, so that from January 2010 users can place up to three hold requests for titles that are already checked out. They can also view their place in line and receive e-mail notification when the book becomes available.

- Some vendors **combine these two models**. *Safari Books Online*, for example, allows libraries to select a number of 'bookshelf' slots per month. Libraries can also swap titles within the slot, if titles are not getting any usage. Safari also offers simultaneous access.

Purchase models also differ widely. E-books may be offered on annual subscriptions, on a lease, as one-off purchases with annual access fees, or as one-off purchases with additional payments for new titles. For example, libraries can only access *Knovel* collections while they are paying for the subscription, whereas *Gale Virtual Reference* books are purchased permanently. *Ebook Library* (*EBL*) offers two models. 'Non-linear Lending' allows for multiple concurrent accesses up to a total of 325 unique uses per year. These permissions renew annually without additional fees from the initial purchase. 'Unlimited Access' allows for unrestricted perpetual access to e-books by an unlimited number of

Figure 3.5 E-Book Universe

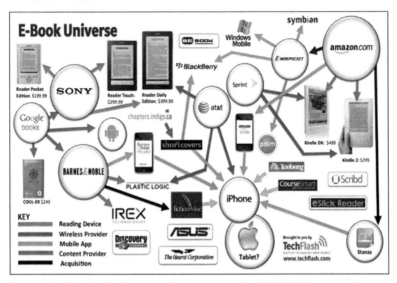

Source: TechFlash *http://www.techflash.com/seattle/2009/09/the_expanding_universe_of_electronic_books.html*

patrons. In addition to purchase models, *EBL* also offers several demand-driven access models including pay-per-view access (mediated or automatic) and auto-purchase.

Some libraries go into individual deals with publishers and vendors, some via consortia. The University of Auckland Library, for example, has mostly individual subscriptions, but also a few that are negotiated via the CONZUL[67] consortium. In the United Kingdom, JISC has funded a collection of over 3,000 multidisciplinary e-books from *ebrary* for over 440 further education colleges. KoBSON, the acquisition consortium of libraries in Serbia, has negotiated access to several e-book collections on the level of the whole country. ERALL (Electronic Resources Academic Library Link) is a consortium formed by the eight university libraries in Hong Kong to purchase collectively e-books in the English language.

When planning for e-book integration, libraries should also bear in mind that, on top of the cost of purchasing collections, they will incur further costs for maintaining collections, and for staff and user training.

Copyright and Digital Rights Management

Copyright and Digital Rights Management have been described in detail by many other authors, including recent publications by Paul Torremans,[68] Neil Netanel,[69] Grace Agnew[70] and Christopher May.[71] Here I will briefly mention these topics as they have huge influence on the provision and use of e-books.

The issues related to managing copyrighted materials are extremely complex. On the one hand, libraries have to provide their patrons with access to copyrighted works and the information and ideas they contain, and, on the other, they have to respect the idea that authors and copyright owners should obtain a fair economic return on their intellectual property. Libraries have to balance between protecting the interests of rights holders and providing access in order to encourage creativity, innovation and research, as well as teaching and learning. This can sometimes be quite tricky.

Copyright is a part of intellectual property law and gives a set of exclusive property rights to owners in relation to their creations. Copyright law creates legal protection for works in any format, including electronic. However, copyright protection for works in electronic format is much more difficult and complex than for works in print format. Among other things, there is the clash between global and local, so often seen in the modern world – access to e-books is global, while copyright laws vary from country to country.

The International Federation of Library Associations' (IFLA) policy on copyright in the digital environment is that digital material is no different from print, and that existing legislation should be extended to the digital environment. In the document *The IFLA Position on Copyright in the Digital Environment*, approved by the IFLA Executive Board in August 2000, IFLA says that information resource sharing 'plays a crucial role in education, democracy, economic growth, health and welfare and personal development', and that 'providing access to a digital format of a protected work to a user for a legitimate purpose such as research or study should be a permitted act under copyright law'. IFLA also argues that legislation should cover the legal deposit of electronic media too.[72]

In addition to copyright, the accessibility and integrity of digital works can also be covered by Digital Rights Management (DRM). The term itself is generic, and is used to describe technologies that are used to control access and impose limitations on the usage of digital content and devices. Digital Rights Management is one of the most critical elements in the world of electronic publishing. It is more complex for e-books than e-journals because of publishers' concerns about possible loss of print revenue. This is especially the case with academic textbooks.

E-book publishers exercise various degrees of control over the access, sharing and lending of intellectual property. This is reflected in the huge number of e-book licensing models. Normally, inter-library loan is not allowed. Some publishers and vendors prefer users to come to them and get e-books on short-term leases rather than to go to borrow them via libraries. However, this is not always possible as the majority of e-books are purchased as part of big packages and not on an individual basis. Publishers also have various practices with regard to the printing, downloading and copying and pasting activities they permit. In some e-book collections these activities are not allowed at all, while others impose various limitations on the numbers of pages that can be printed, downloaded or copied. These restrictions are of critical importance to users. Also, different practices are quite confusing to them.

The complexity and seriousness of the situation for digital material with regard to copyright and DRM can be illustrated by the following example. In April 2008, Oxford University Press, Cambridge University Press and SAGE Publications sued four individuals at Georgia State University, Atlanta. The publishers claimed that the University's e-reserve system was far too liberal, making over 6,700 works available and enabling students to download, view and print these materials without the permission of the copyright holders.[73]

DRM hugely affects interests in all industries related to digital media, including film, music and book publishing. It is often seen as something that prevents lawful fair use of copyrighted works. Publishers are particularly heavily criticised when they put use restrictions on non-copyrighted works that they distribute, such as open-licensed e-books. Because of all the restrictions it imposes, DRM is sometimes called 'Digital Restrictions Management', and anti-DRM groups are even being established all over the world.

Unhappiness with DRM was clearly visible in the *High Wire Press 2009 Librarians eBook Survey and Analysis*.[74] This survey collated the opinions of 138 librarians from thirteen countries. What they liked and disliked about DRM is shown in Table 3.1. The survey shows that the majority of librarians think of the DRM restrictions as either 'unacceptable' or 'somewhat acceptable'. Particularly unpopular were limited length of access and bans on inter-library loans.

DRM restrictions on e-book usage are of critical concern. Current policies are incompatible with the free flow of information needed in the scholarly environment. Libraries would prefer a relaxation of restrictions, to allow perpetual access, classroom use and lending of textual content to other

Table 3.1 Librarians' ratings of DRM restrictions in the 2009 HighWire Press survey

Response	Unacceptable	Somewhat acceptable	Acceptable	Very acceptable	No opinion / Don't know	Total responses
Limited downloading	39	46	19	3	6	113
Limited printing	50	45	8	4	6	113
Limited saving	42	47	15	1	8	113
Limited cut/ paste	54	41	10	2	6	113
Limited length of access	68	18	14	4	6	110
No inter-library loan	61	22	16	4	8	111

libraries. Big changes are needed to enable wider use of e-books and to ensure that e-books do not become just a supplementary reading to their print counterparts. However, publishers' concerns about loss of sales if widespread borrowing becomes the norm are also legitimate.

Content or delivery?

In 2006 I was invited to take part in an e-book forum organised by Ebook Library, James Bennett and Blackwell's Book Services and held prior to the VALA conference in Melbourne, Australia. I was there to represent library opinion. In my talk, of course, I pointed out that libraries need more textbooks published in e-format. The reaction of the publishers' representatives was immediate and vocal: 'Textbooks are our bread and butter.'

The lack of textbooks and core reading in electronic format has been a point of contention between libraries and publishers for many years. Academic libraries would like to be able to provide their users with relevant material. They require e-books which appear on reading lists and support the core curriculum. Students' use of library material is closely tied to course assignments. JISC reports on e-books have shown that students' satisfaction with libraries directly depends on the availability of textbooks in electronic format, and that users need more e-textbooks.[75] On the other hand, print textbooks are a major part of publishers' revenues, and they have been hesitant to risk damaging established markets.

Nevertheless, changes are visible in the e-textbook market too. CourseSmart, an e-textbook company that provides content from a number of scholarly publishers, including Elsevier, Sage, and Taylor & Francis, was founded in 2007. In January 2010 several Internet sites reported that

McGraw-Hill, who have already brought thousands of titles to iPhone and iPod, has started collaborating with Apple on providing e-textbooks on iPad.[76] Amazon has developed its Kindle DX with a large screen, suitable for textbooks, worked out a deal with several textbook publishers to make their material available, and made arrangements with several universities to test the product.

Although it may appear from the above that publishers' attitudes are changing, there are also counter-examples. At the beginning of 2010 one international publisher advised us of their plans not to put any new e-textbooks in their collections. They will not withdraw existing titles, but they will not add any new ones.[77] In a second example, before purchasing a multi-volume book priced at around US $3,000, a colleague sent an e-mail to the publisher enquiring if it was available in an electronic version, and if not, whether there were any plans to make it electronically available in the future. Here is the answer:

> Kind regards,
> All books are available in print edition.
> Due to the increased piracy where publishers are losing $3–4 BILLION each year, we do not plan to have any books in electronic version.[78]

The impact of e-books on library services

The variety of purchase models is seen as a major problem by many librarians. It is often difficult to differentiate between publishers' packages, and to decide whether new books are added to the collection as part of an entitlement or have to be purchased individually. Aggregators and e-book vendors are playing important roles in offering books on the market, but some collections contain books that are part of other collections as well.

A further problem is the fact that the access of e-books and the receipt of bibliographic records for them is not simultaneous. Sometimes a vendor sells the e-book and provides the record before the book is actually available. At other times there is a considerable wait for the vendor to send bibliographic records for books that are already available.

Communication from vendors and publishers to libraries is often poor. Many publishers do not advise on updates to their collections. Repeatedly, libraries have not been notified about ceased or superseded titles or changed URLs. Libraries find this out accidentally, usually when library patrons complain that they cannot access an e-book. It is particularly bad when a lecturer chooses an electronic title for recommended reading and halfway through the course, without any notice, the e-book is no longer available. This gives the impression that e-books are not a reliable resource.

On the other hand, having worked with various vendors over the years I am used to hearing frequent complaints about librarians being inconsistent in their requests. One example would be the definition of necessary MARC fields for e-book records.

Monitoring e-book usage is another difficult area. Not all vendors and publishers provide usage statistics. For libraries with a large number of collections an additional problem is to gather data from different publishers' platforms to get an overview of total e-book usage.

Some of the problems libraries have experienced with freely available e-books result from the fact that publishers of free publications never think of libraries as their customers, nor are they aware of libraries administering access to their e-books. They expect users to come to their web pages to find the needed material, or alternatively, to find it via Google.

Managing freely available e-books is more time-consuming than managing commercial ones. Publishers of free e-books rarely provide bibliographic records. There will be more on this in the next chapter. Here I would just like to point out that many libraries prefer to provide access to e-books via their catalogues, and the lack of bibliographic records means that libraries have to create records themselves.

Publishers and providers often change their web domains, and all the links within bibliographic records in library catalogues cease to work. These publishers do not usually advise libraries of additions or deletions to their collections, which is not surprising, as there is hardly any communication between them and libraries.

This brings up the issue of preserving access to material that libraries would like to keep for historical reasons. Libraries use various methods to ensure that older editions remain available when they are replaced by new ones or withdrawn from websites. All these methods raise issues of copyright and digital rights management.

One option is to make printouts and add them to library print collections. This makes those readers happy who prefer print to digital books, but it also means the library loses any digital copy if the provider withdraws it, and any electronic version will have to be re-digitised. Another option is to store a copy on a library server. This is an easy and cheap option, but only if the library has plenty of storage space and regards the material as valuable enough to administer in a repository. National storage, or a storage facility belonging to a consortium, is also an alternative. All over the world there are examples of various initiatives of this kind. *UK Web Archive*,[79] for example, archives websites and the electronic monographs that are part of them. JISC has a digital preservation and records management programme as part of its activities, whose aim is to ensure that UK universities have continuing access to digital resources created or curated by government, libraries and archives.[80]

Digital storage opens another range of questions and issues. Is the coverage comprehensive? Is the material accessible to anybody, or is it only a deep archive? To that one should add issues with administration and preservation costs.

Over the years libraries have used various tools to manage processes such as acquisition, usage statistics and licences, including spreadsheets, wikis and databases. E-book publishers themselves work continuously on enhancing not only their collections, but also management tools for librarians.

Following the principle of the 'one-stop-shop', SwetsWise has developed its e-books procurement portal as a single source for purchasing e-books, in order to make the process of acquisition easier, and as a means to select the desired access route to their externally sourced content, be it from the publishers directly or via an aggregator.[81] The portal entered into beta testing in November 2009.

ILS vendors also offer products to facilitate management, such as Ex Libris Verde. Serials Solutions offer a complete set of e-resource management and assessment services and these are very popular as a tool for managing serial subscriptions. Since 2008, they have included e-book management in their 360 Resource Manager.

However, the management of e-books remains complex. Many libraries still prefer to put off implementation because of the difficulties involved and are waiting for various issues to be resolved. Libraries that have implemented e-book collections often complain that dealing with e-books requires too much time. The question of whether e-books are giving value for money is continually raised.

The management of e-books is often compared to the management of print books. One common expectation is that e-books will simplify acquisition and management compared to print books. However, the two media are very different. E-books have opened up new possibilities, and realising that, libraries not only started to like e-books, but began to ask vendors and publishers to develop solutions that would help them take advantage of them. So it would be only fair to say that part of the e-book confusion is due to conflicting requests from libraries. On the other hand, e-book vendors and publishers often offer more than their products can deliver. They advertise and present their collections as something that enables seamless integration into libraries. That might be true for their particular collections, but libraries have other collections too.

Maybe our expectations are not realistic and not appropriate for the current level of technology. Maybe the problem is that we expect new technology to be capable of doing anything we would like. Technology is developing rapidly and we are amazed by new developments every day, but often we forget how many times we have been in a position to see that some software or hardware is actually only 'wishware'. The future development of scholarly e-books is very much dependent on both academic libraries and publishers, and on their willingness to cooperate and find solutions that suit them both.

Notes and references

1. Miller, S. (2009) 'The Charleston Conference', *Publishing the Long Civil Rights Movement*. Retrieved 2 July 2010 from *http://lcrm.unc.edu/index.php/2009/11/12/the-charleston-conference*.
2. Vasileiou, M., Hartley, R. and Rowley, J. (2009) 'An overview of the e-book marketplace', *Online Information Review*, 33(1).

3. See *http://www.idpf.org/doc_library/industrystats.htm*.

4. Nelson, M. R. (2008) *E-Books in Higher Education: Nearing the End of the Era of Hype?* Research Bulletin, 2008. Retrieved 2 July 2010 from *http://www.educause. edu/ECAR/EBooksinHigherEducationNearing/162438*.

5. 'E-books in Japan: distribution, use and preservation' (2009) *National Diet Library Newsletter*, 169. Retrieved 2 July 2010 from *http://www.ndl.go.jp/en/publication/ ndl_newsletter/169/691.html*.

6. 'China eBook Market Development Report: 79 million readers' (22 April 2009) *Web2Asia*. Retrieved 2 July 2010 from *http://www.web2asia.com/2009/04/22/2008-china-ebook-market-development-report#permalink*.

7. 'E-book sales to explode in China' (2010, 21 January) *People's Daily Online*. Retrieved 2 July 2010 from *http://english.peopledaily.com.cn/90001/90778/90860/ 6861670.html*.

8. Ho, S. (20 January 2010) 'E-book industry in Taiwan shines in 2010 Taipei International Book Exhibition', *EBook Forum*. Retrieved 2 July 2010 from *http:// ebookforum.wordpress.com/2010/01/20/e-book-industry-in-taiwan-shines-in-2010-taipei-international-book-exhibition/*.

9. Cox, J. and Cox, L. (2010) *Scholarly Book Publishing Practice: An ALPSP Survey of Academic Book Publishers' Policies and Practices, First Survey, 2009*. Shoreham-by-Sea: Association of Learned and Professional Society Publishers.

10. Aptara is a US-based company founded in 1988, which provides integrated content transformation services and solutions.

11. *Aptara Survey Reveals Publishers' Evolving Response to eBooks: First in a Series of Surveys Documenting the Impact of New Media on Book Publishing Operations*.

(2010) Retrieved 2 July 2010 from *http://www.aptaracorp. com/images/pdf/Aptara_eBook_survey_1.pdf.*

12. See *http://books.google.com/googlebooks/agreement/#5.*

13. Sandoval, G. (18 February 2010) 'Google book settlement draws fire in court', *CNET news.* Retrieved 2 July 2010 from *http://news.cnet.com/8301-31001_3-10456382-261.html.*

14. Drummond, D. (5 February 2010) 'Google: we will bring books back to life', *Guardian.co.uk.* Retrieved 6 July 2010 from *http://www.guardian.co.uk/commentisfree/ 2010/feb/05/google-bringing-books-back-life.*

15. McGrath, M. (2010) 'Interlending and document supply: a review of the recent literature', No 71. *Interlending and Document Supply,* 38(2).

16. Johnson, L., Levine, A., Smith, R. and Stone, S. (2010) *The 2010 Horizon Report.* Retrieved 2 July 2010 from *http://www.educause.edu/ELI/2010HorizonReport/ 195400.*

17. 'Development platform accelerates eBook market introduction: new eBook development platform based on TI's OMAP(TM) 3 technology speeds time to market, lowers costs for eBook manufacturers' (19 January 2010). [Electronic Version]. *Product News Network.* Retrieved 23 January 2010 from *http://metalib.auckland.ac .nz:80/V/49FM171H4TVQ3JH5TPYTA86MFHRV CQMEH1EJHR56KJJQ913U8A02756?FUNC percent 3DLATERAL percent2DLINK percent26DOC percent 5FNUMBER percent3D000132514 percent26LINE percent5FNUMBER percent3D0007.*

18. Ibid.

19. See *http://www.apple.com/ipad/specs/.*

20. Aptara (2010) 'iPad: what does it really mean for content publishers?' Retrieved 2 July 2010 from *http://www. aptaracorp.com/index.php?/ipad.html.*

21. See *http://www.lawcom.govt.nz/Publications.aspx*.

22. See *http://www.lawcom.gov.uk/lc_reports.htm*.

23. See *http://lawcommissionofindia.nic.in/reports.htm*.

24. See *http://www.gutenberg.org/wiki/Main_Page*.

25. See *www.archive.org*.

26. See *http://www.free-ebooks.net/* .

27. Posted on 17 January 2010 at *http://ebooksonlinefree. blogspot.com*.

28. See *http://www.e-book.com.au/*.

29. See *http://www.onlinecourses.org/2009/11/11/100-useful-links-for-ebook-lovers/*.

30. See *http://digital.library.upenn.edu/books/*.

31. See *http://www.authorama.com/*.

32. See *http://www.planetebook.com/*.

33. See *http://www.aozora.gr.jp/*.

34. Mugridge, R.L. (2006) 'Managing digitization activities', *SPEC Kit* Vol. 294. Retrieved 2 July 2010 from *http://www.arl.org/bm~doc/spec294web.pdf*.

35. *ebrary's Global eBook Survey* (2007) Retrieved 14 January, 2010, from *http://www.ebrary.com/corp/collateral/en/Survey/ebrary_eBook_survey_2007.pdf*.

36. Primary Research Group (2008) *Library Use of E-books*, 2008–09 edn. New York: Primary Research Group, p. 23.

37. Lampert, C. and Vaughan, J. (2009) 'Success factors and strategic planning: rebuilding an academic library digitization program', *Information Technology and Libraries*, September, 116–136.

38. Collection is available at *www.enzb.auckland.ac.nz/*.

39. Laurie, J. (2006) *Reviving the Past: The Early New Zealand Books Online Project at the University of Auckland Library*. Paper presented at the VALA 2006. Retreived 2 July 2010 from *http://www.valaconf.org.au/vala2006/papers2006/19_Laurie_Final.pdf*.

40. See *http://www.letrs.indiana.edu/web/w/wright2/*.

41. See *http://www.hathitrust.org/*.

42. Available from *http://www.ulib.org*.

43. See *http://search.theeuropeanlibrary.org/portal/en/index. html*.

44. See *http://www.wdl.org/en/about/faq.html*.

45. Lynch, C.A. (2003) *Institutional Repositories: Essential Infrastructure for Scholarship in the Digital Age.* ARL, 266. Retrieved 2 July 2010 from *http://www.arl.org/ resources/pubs/br/br226/br226ir.shtml*.

46. Hall, G. (2008) *Digitize This Book! The Politics of New Media, or Why We Need Open Access Now.* Minneapolis: University of Minnesota Press.

47. Swan, A. (2010) *The Open Access Citation Advantage: Studies and Results to Date.* School of Electronics and Computer Science, University of Southampton.

48. Smith, M. et al. (2003) 'DSpace: an open source dynamic digital repository' [electronic version], *D-Lib Magazine,* 9(1), retrieved 2 July 2010 from *http://webdoc.sub .gwdg.de/edoc/aw/d-lib/dlib/january03/smith/01smith. html*.

49. Davis, P.M. and Connolly, M.J.L. (2007) 'Institutional repositories: evaluating the reasons for non-use of Cornell University's installation of DSpace [electronic version], *D-Lib Magazine,* 13(3/4). Retrieved 2 July 2010 from *http://works.bepress.com/cgi/viewcontent.cgi?article= 1007&context=ir_research*.

50. See *http://dspace.mit.edu/*.

51. See *http://escholarship.org/*.

52. Hayes, L., Stevenson, A., Mason, I., Scott, A. and Kennedy, P. (2007) 'Institutional collaboration around institutional repositories' [electronic version]. Retrieved 24 January 2010, from *http://researchspace.auckland. ac.nz/handle/2292/411*.

53. See *http://researchspace.auckland.ac.nz/handle/2292/4486*.

54. Fox, E.A. et al. (1996) 'National Digital Library of Theses and Dissertations' [electronic version], *D-Lib Magazine*. Retrieved 2 July 2010 from *http://www.dlib.org/dlib/september96/theses/09fox.html*.

55. See *http://www.ndltd.org/*.

56. Andrew, T. (2004) 'Intellectual property and electronic theses' [electronic version], *JISC Legal Information*, September. Retrieved 12 December 2009 from *http://www.era.lib.ed.ac.uk/bitstream/1842/612/2/IP_etheses.pdf*.

57. See *http://adt.caul.edu.au/*.

58. Copeland, S., Penman, A. and Milne, R. (2005) 'Electronic theses: the turning point', *Program: Electronic Library and Information Systems*, 39(3), 185–197.

59. For more information on EThoS at *http://ethos.bl.uk/Home.do*.

60. Snowhill, L. (2001) 'E-books and their future in academic libraries: an overview', *D-Lib Magazine*, 7(7/8).

61. '10 steps to implementing eBook collections: a guide for librarians', (2007). Retrieved 14 January 2010 from *http://www.springer.com/cda/content/document/cda_downloaddocument/10steps_ebook.pdf?SGWID=0-0-45-686398-0*.

62. Boehm, Ron. (2008) 'The economics of publishing and eBook', *No Shelf Required*. Retrieved 2 July 2010 from *http://www.libraries.wright.edu/noshelfrequired/?page_id=5*.

63. Ibid.

64. Ganapati, P. (2009) 'Kindle readers ignite protest over e-book prices', *Gadget Lab*, 6 April 2009. Retrieved 2 July 2010 from *http://www.wired.com/gadgetlab/2009/04/kindle-readers*.

65. *ebrary's Global eBook Survey* (2007) Retrieved 14 January, 2010, from *http://www.ebrary.com/corp/collateral/en/Survey/ebrary_eBook_survey_2007.pdf*.

66. Renner, R.A. (2007) *eBooks – Costs and Benefits to Academic and Research Libraries.* Retrieved 7 February 2010 from *http://www.springer.com/cda/content/document/cda_downloaddocument/eBook+White+Paper.pdf?SGWID=0-0-45-415198-0.*

67. CONZUL is the Council of New Zealand University Librarians and acts collectively for the common benefit of New Zealand universities.

68. Torremans, P. (2007) *Copyright Law: A Handbook of Contemporary Research.* Cheltenham, UK and Northampton, MA: Edward Elgar.

69. Netanel, N. (2008) *Copyright's Paradox.* Oxford and New York: Oxford University Press.

70. Agnew, G. (2008) *Digital Rights Management: A Librarian's Guide to Technology and Practice.* Oxford: Chandos.

71. May, C. (2007) *Digital Rights Management: The Problem of Expanding Ownership Rights.* Oxford: Chandos.

72. The IFLA Position on Copyright in the Digital Environment is available from *http://archive.ifla.org/III/clm/p1/pos-dig.htm* (accessed 2 July 2010).

73. Albanese, A. (2010, 11 March) 'Both sides angle for victory in key e-reserve copyright case', *Library Journal.* Retrieved 2 July 2010 from *http://www.libraryjournal.com/article/CA6722663.html.*

74. Newman, M. (2010) *HighWire Press 2009 Librarian eBook Survey.* Retrieved 2 July 2010 from *http://highwire.stanford.edu/PR/HighWireEBookSurvey2010.pdf.*

75. JISC (2009) *JISC National E-book Observatory Project: Key Findings and Recommendations: Final Report*, November 2009.

76. Ante, S.E. (2010) 'Apple in talks with McGraw-Hill, Hachette over Tablet', *Business Week*, 27 January 2010. Retrieved 28 January 2010 from *http://www.businessweek. com/technology/content/jan2010/tc20100121_ 991806.htm*.

77. From a conversation with publisher's representative.

78. These two publishers have chosen not to be identified.

79. See *http://www.webarchive.org.uk/ukwa/info/about#what_ uk_archive*.

80. More about this programme can be found at *http:// www.jisc.ac.uk/whatwedo/programmes/preservation. aspx*.

81. Gisbergen, M.V. (2009) 'eBooks – a platform to build on', *Serials: The Journal for the Serials Community*, 22(3), S11.

4

Developing and managing e-book collections

Academic libraries are steadily shifting from print to electronic resources. Many assign more than half their budgets to e-content. The University of New South Wales Library, for example, spends 75 per cent.[1] Association of Research Libraries (ARL) statistics for 2007 and 2008 show that the average ARL university library spends 51 per cent of its materials budget on electronic resources. Some libraries allocate more than 80 per cent of their budgets to electronic resources.[2]

The Primary Research Group survey shows that United States libraries spent an average of 25.4 per cent more on e-books in 2007 than in 2006, and an average of 36 per cent more in 2008 than in 2007. E-book spending by non United States libraries that participated in the survey increased by almost 90 per cent in 2007.[3]

Integrated library systems (ILSs) have failed to keep up with this trend. They are designed to handle cataloguing, circulation and acquisition functions for print collections and they are not adequate for effectively managing electronic material. To support administration of electronic collections independent and proprietary electronic resource management (ERM) systems have been developed – some commercially, some built in-house.

Products like Ex Libris Verde and Serials Solutions 360 Resource Manager are becoming popular. However, they still do not offer comprehensive administration of e-books as they cover neither all e-books nor all aspects of e-book management. Together with ILSs they are part of the very complex infrastructure libraries have to support in the background.

The Kuali OLE initiative[4] is interesting in this context. Open Library Environment (OLE) is defined as a next-generation technology environment. It has been developed as an alternative to the current Integrated Library System model. The software is supposed to manage the complex business processes and workflow of academic libraries in the digital age. More than 300 libraries, educational institutions, professional organisations and businesses participated in some phase of the planning for the OLE project, which was supported by a planning grant from the Andrew W. Mellon Foundation and led by Duke University. The OLE Project Final Report was published in October 2009, and is available from the website. It gives an overview of the project and a timeline. Software development was planned to begin in January 2010. OLE software is expected to be able to replace an existing ILS in mid 2012.[5]

The e-book environment is pretty much unstable and unpredictable. Because of this it is difficult to create and apply an e-book collection development policy. According to the 2009 Association of Research Libraries (ARL) survey, 82 per cent of responding libraries do not specifically mention e-books in their collection development policies.[6] This is because collection development policies have been content-driven, and most e-book purchases are not content-related.

Libraries have used a variety of approaches in deploying electronic collections. The options they have chosen very much depend on the size of their e-book collections. Libraries with only a few e-book collections face far fewer problems than libraries with huge collections. However, even libraries with one or two packages say that e-books are complex and difficult to manage. For libraries with sixty, seventy or more purchased and leased collections, and further collections of free e-books, managing e-books remains a real challenge.

The next section describes some of the options, and I hope it will help tertiary libraries buying their first e-books to make decisions that are right for them.

Selection and purchasing

A number of purchasing models are offered to libraries, including subscription (similar to e-journal subscription), pay-per-view, 'bundled' (often subject-based collections), and patron-driven acquisition where purchases are made only when a specific title is accessed. New purchasing models continue to emerge, as vendors and publishers try to find options that would be suitable for different kinds of libraries. For example, *Ebook Library (EBL)* offers on-demand selection as an answer to a common complaint that libraries often end up taking everything publishers offer. This model enables libraries to buy individual titles that they actually need.

ebrary's Global eBook Survey[7] found that purchase and subscription were the two most preferred models (Figure 4.1). Librarians were asked to select all models that applied and some of them selected both. Allen McKiel, Director of Libraries, Northeastern State University, who analysed the survey, gives the following explanation for this choice:

> The preference for either the subscription model or the purchase model in my view depends primarily on the content needs of the institutions. It is reasonable to associate control of access to and specific selection of

content as motivations associated with respondents who prefer the purchase model. Quantity and breadth of content are likely motivators associated with the subscription model. I suspect that institutions which are heavily research centred have a stronger need for specificity than those focused more on teaching and general education. In either case, content concerns are primary with price determining the model for optimising access to quantity.[8]

In the same survey, the patron-driven model, pay-per-use and lease-to-own were much less popular. McKiel suspects that the reason for this is a lack of familiarity with the models as options in the content/price optimisation calculation.

Figure 4.1 Preferred acquisition mode in ebrary's *Global eBook Survey*

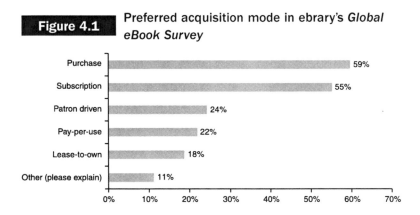

In 2007, the Council of Australian University Librarians surveyed its members on e-book purchasing. With regard to acquisition methods, subscriptions to collections were most popular, followed by individual title purchase, collection purchase and individual title subscriptions. In the report about the survey, Colleen Cleary notes that

whilst the prevalence of a particular purchase model amongst the survey responses might potentially indicate a preference, this may also be determined by the products and purchase models available.[9]

The survey also indicated that respondents sought flexibility to choose between purchase models, and that many libraries have a mix of different purchasing models, depending on the content.

A 2009 ARL survey also highlights the fact that e-book selection is tightly linked to vendor options. In this survey collection and title-by-title purchasing are equally popular. More libraries prefer to own content than to lease it, except in the case of frequently updated titles and rapidly changing subject areas.[10]

Libraries that purchase only one or two collections find that e-book packages make bulk ordering more efficient. However, generally, the variety of purchase models is a major problem for librarians as they cannot streamline the selection process. Inefficient and diverse order processes make ordering e-books more complicated and time-consuming than print.

Some libraries have made attempts to integrate e-books into approval plans, as that would bring print and e-book acquisition into one process, reduce duplication of titles and provide better control of purchasing. Challenges facing this approach have been described by Michael Levine-Clark, including lack of frontlist titles, lack of a sustainable pricing model, the multiplicity of e-book vendors, and the reluctance of some publishers to make their content available at all. He describes several solutions, but points out that, for e-books to be really integrated into the approval process, a significant number of frontlist titles have to be available at the time of publication.[11]

The traditional separation of finances for books and serials is blurring. E-books are often bought from serials funds because of the need to budget for ongoing commitments. The acquisition of e-books is frequently handled by serials departments. E-books are offered in packages similar to e-serial packages, and may even be combined with e-journal content on the same platform. Barbara Dunham and Trish Davis, who did a review of the literature on acquisitions from 2004 through 2007, say that acquiring electronic resources is simpler than managing them effectively.[12]

Before they make a recommendation to purchase a new e-book collection, librarians need to consider a number of issues. Below is the checklist compiled for subject librarians at the University of Auckland Library. The list was made several years ago with the aim of helping subject librarians make decisions on whether or not to purchase e-book collections:

Platform

1. What kind of document format is your e-book in (i.e. html, xml, PDF, proprietary)?
2. How do you navigate through the pages?
3. Is it web based or do you need client software?
4. Do you support stable title-level jumpstarts (i.e. can we link from our catalogue to a URL for an individual book)?
5. Do you supply MARC records with embedded URLs?

Readers

1. Do you need any readers to view the content?
2. Are they proprietary to your product? (Important.)
3. If yes to 2. – How often do you send updates for the readers?

Borrowing

1. Describe how our users borrow or view books.
2. How much can they print?

3. If you have to create an account, how do you keep track of users who may have left the university?

4. If buying sets of e-books, can our users retrieve a customised bookshelf or list of works to which they have access?

Authentication

1. Can it be IP based?

2. Does it work with ezproxy?

3. If you use a password or other methods, please describe. Note: access needs to be networkable, not single PC-based.

Future of the product

1. What other vendors are you affiliated with?

2. Is your e-book line subject based?

Many other libraries also developed guidelines on e-book selection. Guidelines developed by various ARL member libraries have been published in *E-book collections*.[13]

Providing access

There are two main approaches to enabling users to get to the full text – remote access, and providing e-books via e-book readers.

Remote access

Access via the web to the vendor or publisher database, seems to be preferred by the majority of libraries. It has many advantages. It enables 24/7 access, i.e. content is always accessible, regardless of time or space, which is a crucial consideration for universities that provide distance education. Libraries also save server space, since they don't have to store the e-books themselves, and they don't have to maintain the database.

There is a downside too. Libraries have to provide sufficient PCs on campus, as well as having authentication systems in place to enable access to the fee-based websites the libraries subscribe to. The system has to recognise users from the university campus, as well as from other places they might want to connect from.

Libraries provide various ways of accessing e-books via their websites. The predominant methods are:

- Web lists of e-book databases, which can be arranged alphabetically, or by subject or type. Users go directly to publisher servers, to the home page of the collection they have selected. Once in the collection, readers have the advantage of full-text searches across the whole collection or individual books within it. Most e-book databases have administration features which allow usage data, such as popular books and topics of high interest, to be identified and graphed. Readers can create personal files, add notes to the margins of e-books and make shortcuts to favourite books. The databases have other features too, like inbuilt dictionaries, and audio files that pronounce words in the texts.

  The drawback of this access is that readers can perform searches only within one collection, and not across all library e-book resources. Also, static web pages can be labour-intensive to maintain.

- Most academic libraries offer research guides on their websites. These may be targeted at major subject areas, or specific university courses. Often librarians include e-books in lists of readings for particular courses. Subject guides include both pathfinders and reference guides. Pathfinders tend to be shorter and more focused on helping students start on their research, while reference guides are longer and more comprehensive. At the University of Auckland Library, subject librarians create course pages for individual courses taught at the University. These pages have lists of print and electronic resources with direct links to individual e-books.

Research guides are easy and convenient for students, and save them significant amounts of time they would have to spend on locating relevant resources. They also optimise investment in e-resources and provide students with a fully-interlinked information environment, which is the work environment they expect.

As with database lists on web pages, research guides need constant updating, so they don't become inconsistent and incomplete, with incorrect metadata and broken links.

■ Bibliographic records in the library catalogue enable users to search the entire range of library resources, print and electronic. Catalogue records contain URL links to full e-book content. Metadata within the catalogue is pre-indexed, so the searches are very fast. However, this search is comprehensive only if the library has catalogued all its e-books.

Limiting a catalogue search to electronic books can be a difficult task for students, but it is possible with some library systems. Several ARL member libraries have their catalogue searches limited to e-books. Anson and Connell give snapshots of catalogues for Duke University, University of North Carolina at Chapel Hill, Pennsylvania State University, Vanderbilt University and Washington State University in *E-book collections*.[14] The University of Auckland Library has also created a canned search on its

Voyager catalogue. Search limits are based on the codes 'a' and 'm' in the Leader Line (000, positions 6 and 7) in the bibliographic record, and on the location code for electronic material in the holding record. However, the Library plans to have only Primo discovery layer and to remove Voyager OPAC. Primo post-search faceting will enable users to narrow their search to electronic books.

A fully-interlinked information environment can be achieved by combining catalogue and database search results in a single set. Unfortunately, simultaneous searches of library catalogues and e-book databases remain unsatisfactory. They can be labour-intensive to set up. Simultaneous searching is slower, and this is certainly not something that users want. There is also an issue with practical limits to the number of databases that can be searched at once. The order of search results can be confusing, and there are many problems with varying formats and field structures in results displays. A further disadvantage is that every search performed this way may be counted by the vendor as a usage session of the resource, and give a false impression of usage. This is particularly impractical for databases that allow only a limited number of concurrent users.

Other issues with federated searches are the possibility of retrieving the same book from the catalogue and the database because of duplicated metadata, reconciling varying subject thesauri, and searching sources with only subject headings at the same time as sources with abstracts or full text.

Products like SFX can also provide searches across multiple databases. These searches cover only electronic resources, but users save a significant amount of time by searching journal articles and e-books concurrently. Unfortunately, these searches still do not include all e-books, or even all electronic resources. Any material that is not purchased as a part of a database cannot be accessed via metasearch, so users again get an incomplete picture.

Search platforms such as Primo or VuFind combine metadata records from different repositories with catalogue metadata, and enable searches across all the library's resources. They can also harvest content from other platforms. An example of incorporating *Internet Archive* content into VuFind is described by Eric Lease Morgan in the *Infomotions Mini-Musings* blog.[15] There are also examples of adding records to Primo from HathiTrust. The University of Waterloo added records for over 250,000 e-books. Because of Primo's ability to add metadata from an unlimited number of repositories, they expect Primo to continue to grow and include indexing for other repositories of research interest.[16] OCLC's WorldCat Local is another initiative worth mentioning in this context as it combines a central database index of library resources and article databases with a search of non-OCLC content indexed remotely.[17]

The method a library chooses to provide remote access very much depends on the number and size of its e-book collections. Dinkelman and Stacy-Bates say that it is crucial that library websites provide various pathways for easy access.[18] Most libraries opt for a variety of methods, and thus ensure their readers find their e-books no matter where their searches start from.

University of Auckland Library usage statistics confirm that providing users only with access to vendors' and publishers' servers is not enough. Figure 4.2 shows the preferences of the University of Auckland users. It gives the number of user sessions for the three most popular e-book collections for the period from January to December 2009. The Library has created

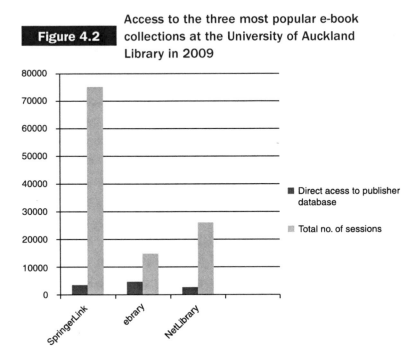

Figure 4.2 Access to the three most popular e-book collections at the University of Auckland Library in 2009

individual gateway pages for all its e-book collections, called Connect Pages. The table compares the traffic from Connect Pages, as counted by the Library, with numbers of user sessions as supplied by vendors. Unfortunately, there is no data to show where the traffic reported by vendors comes from. However, we can presume with a good level of certainty that the Library catalogue, Google Scholar and Scirus[19] figure prominently.

This corresponds with the findings of the E-book Focus Group[20] and many others. *ebrary's Global eBook Survey* (see Figure 4.3), for example, shows that the library catalogue 'is still the centre of the information universe'[21] but that other methods of access, although ranked lower than library OPACs, still appear to be powerful tools.

Despite its popularity, remote access has not gone without criticism. An often heard complaint is the problem of portability – that it is not easy to take a PC, or even a laptop

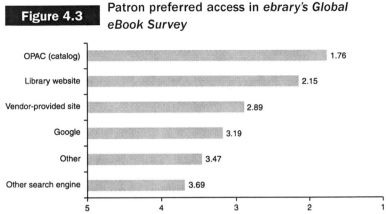

Figure 4.3 Patron preferred access in *ebrary's Global eBook Survey*

Note: Each item was rated on a scale of 1 to 5, where 1 = most common and 5 = least common.

with you wherever you go. They are heavy compared to print books or e-book readers and their screens are not easy on readers' eyes.

Dedicated e-book readers

Portable readers very much imitate the print-book model – books must be issued to users, and returned. While some authors think that this method brings more problems than benefits, others argue that the process is technically easy to solve, and that it is not difficult to work out methods to control access and enable users to download e-books from publishers' sites at their own convenience. However, not all vendors and publishers are ready for this at this time. Furthermore, e-book readers vary in their performances and in the formats they support. Table 4.1 offers a comparison of two popular readers, Kindle 2 and Sony. The lack of standard reading devices means that libraries would be limited to the e-book collections that are compatible with the e-readers they choose.

Table 4.1	Comparison of Kindle 2 and Sony Reader PRS-700BC

	Kindle 2	Sony Reader PRS-700 BC
Size	8" × 5.3" × 0.36"	5.1" × 6.7" × 0.40"
Thickness	0.36"	0.40"
Weight	10.2 oz	10 oz. (without soft cover)
Display	6" display with no touch screen. 600× 800 pixel resolution at 167 pixels per inch, 16-level grey scale that offers better contrast.	6" touch screen display, 600 × 800 pixel resolution at 170 pixels per inch, 8-level grey scale
Connectivity	Wireless connectivity using Sprint's data network to search and download books, no Wi-Fi	None. Connectivity via USB port to Internet-enabled PC
Storage	2GB memory that supports about 1,500 books.	512 MB standard with expansion using Sony Memory Stick Duo Pro and SDHC card. Standard storage supports about 350 books.
Formats supported	Kindle, text, Audible, MP3, PDF, HTML, DOC, Images	DRM text, MP3, PDF, DOC, Images
Price	$360	$400
Colours	White	Silver, Black, Red
Audio	Text to speech that allows for the book to be read out loud. Which means your can turn it on and have it read Dr Seuss out loud to the kids or a bedtime story for you.	None
Extras	Basic web browser that allows for access to text-centric sites including access to Wikipedia and Google among others	None

Source: http://www.wired.com/gadgetlab/2009/02/showdown-kindle.

The main advantages of dedicated readers are their portability and screen readability in bright sunlight. Manufacturers continue to produce new models and improve existing models. Reading devices are becoming more advanced. They are lighter and thinner (Figure 4.4 shows Kindle 2 compared to a pencil) and have much longer battery life. Most e-readers today use an electronic ink display that consumes very l ittle power and makes reading easier. Many e-readers support wireless downloads over 3G, and some come with a basic Internet browser. Some have touchscreens for note-making and marking, and inbuilt text-to-speech conversion.

On the other hand, with new models continually appearing, older models become clunky and obsolete. For example, Rocket Ebook reader production stopped in 2003. Most e-book readers support only the basic formats of PDF, HTML, text, MP3 and JPEG. The popular Amazon Kindle 2, for example, does not

Figure 4.4   **Amazon Kindle 2 e-book reader**

Source: From Amazon.com/Kindle.

support open book formats. This reader is deliberately limited to Amazon books, and not really usable in the academic environment. Several Internet sites give comparisons of e-book readers, for example *ebook 88*[22] or *Top Ten Reviews*.[23] Wiley has also launched an e-reader comparison site.[24]

Another significant disadvantage in the academic environment is that e-readers, with the exception of CourseSmart, offer no way to integrate EndNote or similar bibliographic citation systems. Nor do they support colour, or the special features found in scientific e-books. The Primary Research Group survey on library use of e-books shows that just over 10 per cent of the libraries in the sample owned any kind of e-book reading device that was not a traditional computer workstation.[25]

Nevertheless, some universities prefer e-book readers to web access. The main reason, according to John Rodzvilla, is the fact that e-readers 'offer patrons the portability of a traditional print book but with the ability to access entire on-line libraries,' and also that they are a possible solution to eye-strain problems and computer vision syndrome.[26]

Dan D'Agostino criticises academic libraries for their current practices:

> Instead of focusing on books downloadable to e-readers or smart phones, academic libraries have created enormous databases of e-books that students and faculty members can read only on computer screens.[27]

D'Agostino also asks:

> With a vigorous, searchable Google Books on the horizon, could academic libraries suddenly find themselves and their e-book collections completely bypassed by their students and faculty?[28]

Penn State University Libraries are working in collaboration with Sony Electronics, Inc. to investigate how the Sony Reader Digital Book works in the academic library and university environments.[29]

In 2009 Amazon.com sponsored a pilot programme for its large-screen Kindle DX e-reader across seven university colleges: the University of Virginia, Arizona State University, Case Western Reserve University, Princeton University, Reed College, Pace University and the University of Washington. The goals of the pilot were to see if e-readers were suitable for use in university classes, to discover their strengths and weaknesses compared to traditional content delivery, and to find ways of reducing the cost. At the time of writing this book, the only feedback from this trial has come from Princeton University. At this university, students in three courses were given a reader containing their course readings for the fall semester. 'But though they acknowledged some benefits of the new technology, many students and faculty in the three courses said they found the Kindles disappointing and difficult to use.'[30] Many of them said they were dissatisfied and uncomfortable with the devices.

Apple's iPad has been seen as something that can become the learning device of the future. Three United States universities – Seton Hill University, George Fox University and Abilene Christian University – have announced their plans to pilot iPads in classrooms. They also intend to train teachers to integrate mobile web software and iPad apps into their curricula.[31] However, the tablet has been rejected by George Washington University and Princeton University because of network stability issues. Cornell University also expressed their reservation with regard to problems with connectivity and bandwidth overload.[32]

Another issue of concern for the tertiary education institutions is Apple's initiatives in the provision of textbooks and whether textbook publishers will sign deals with Apple. CourseSmart has already announced an iPad app.[33] CourseSmart is a subscription-based service that charges fees for students to access e-textbooks of their choice for a limited time. The company offers access to about 10,000 e-textbooks and includes titles from the five biggest textbook publishers. The demo of the CourseSmart app is available on YouTube.[34] McGraw-Hill, Houghton Mifflin, Pearson and Kaplan have made deals with software developer ScrollMotion to develop iPad-friendly versions of textbooks.[35]

Apart from dedicated e-book readers, other devices can be used for reading electronic books, such as Personal Digital Assistants (PDA), and mobile phones. Terena Solomons describes the use of therapeutic guidelines and medical textbooks downloaded on PDAs at the Hollywood Private Hospital.[36] In an environment like this, having the necessary drug and clinical reference information, together with patients' details and the history of their illnesses on a portable device, is more practical than access via the Internet.

Using mobile phones to read e-books is becoming increasingly popular all over the world. In China, for example, the growth of the mobile reading business was 117 per cent in 2007 thanks to a continuing decrease in call charges and the increased availability of large-screen phones and smart-phones, which have enhanced the performance, function, speed, capacity and popularity of mobile reading.[37]

There are many examples of the successful application of mobile technology in education.[38] One argument in favour is that students already have mobile phones with wireless access to the Internet, and that they already use them for reading. So, rather than purchasing another device, students can download learning materials, e-books and course material on their existing mobiles.

Generally speaking, libraries are not in a position to choose the way they will provide e-books, but have to go on with what is available on the e-book market.

In 2009 the Association of Learned and Professional Society Publishers (ALPSP) conducted a survey of academic book publishers' policies and practices. The survey was sent to 400 publishers, and over 60 per cent answered. The findings were published in the *Scholarly Book Publishing Practice Report* in 2010. The survey showed that the majority of publishers are providing e-books for PCs and laptops; 18.6 per cent provide e-books for dedicated e-book readers, 9.3 per cent for PDA and 4.1 per cent for mobile phones (Figure 4.5). The survey also found that commercial publishers used e-book readers and experimented with different reading devices more than non-profit publishers. Experimentation increased with size – probably due to the costs involved.[39]

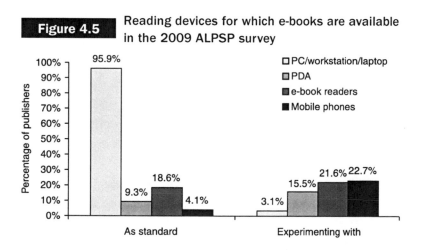

Figure 4.5 Reading devices for which e-books are available in the 2009 ALPSP survey

Bibliographic records

It is expected that a librarian will emphasise the value of bibliographic records, even more so someone like me, who is the manager of a cataloguing unit. But non-librarians have also recognised their value. Dean Mason, business development manager and editor of a number of books on digital publishing, calls the cataloguing record 'an intelligent agent of exchange',[40] and says,

> Although perhaps not yet acknowledged as such, the cataloguing record has arguably become the one unit of information exchange that information consumers require for universal meaning to be injected into the amorphous world of the Internet.[41]

The need for standardised high-quality metadata is even more highlighted in the increasingly popular 'centralised source of discovery' model.

Currently, the most popular format for bibliographic records is MARC, and the common practice is to store bibliographic records in individual library catalogues. Both the MARC format and library catalogues have been heavily criticised as unfit for the current needs of the information world. Some changes in cataloguing practices have already been implemented but future directions are uncertain. However, changes in cataloguing practices are not the topic of this book, so I will not go into any speculations about the future of catalogues and cataloguing.

As inventories of collections held by a library, catalogues are useful management tools for reference and acquisitions staff. They enable staff involved in the selection of new material to quickly determine if an item is already held. The absence of a MARC record in the library catalogue can lead to an order being duplicated, and a consequent waste of library funds and staff time.

Enabling access to e-books via library catalogues is important for e-book discovery. There are many reports of increases in e-book usage after records were added to the catalogue, for example by JISC,[42] Dillon,[43] Connaway and Snyder,[44] and Rossmann et al.[45] A particularly interesting example is provided by the *SpringerLink* collection. Springer is a publisher which has recognised the value of MARC records, had them created, and has closely monitored usage of their e-books in relation to the MARC records for them. In *eBooks – the end user perspective*, they report that usage of the *SpringerLink* collection doubled after libraries loaded records to their catalogues.[46] Although their first records were in MARC format, they did not comply with MARC standards and AACR2, so Springer engaged OCLC to create improved MARC records for them. I was told by a Springer representative that usage increased even more after libraries replaced Springer MARC records with OCLC MARC records.

There is no question that MARC records improve e-books discovery, but issues around them are various and complex. Many different approaches have been taken by both libraries and vendors, and today we have a mixture of different practices.

Most commercial publishers and vendors supply MARC records. Unfortunately they do not always understand the principles of bibliographic description and the records they supply are often not good-quality records. Mistakes in these records are frequent and varied. I will mention just a few. Vendors and publishers often re-use records for print books and do not delete elements within the records that are unique, such as Library of Congress Numbers, OCLC Numbers and ISBNs. This creates huge problems for automatic matching of bibliographic data. Sometimes records are coded in a way which the ILSs cannot recognise at all, so the records cannot be loaded, or if they load, diacritics display incorrectly. In some extreme cases publishers have sent records for print editions without changing them at all, and without even adding URLs to link to the electronic editions.

There are still publishers who do not provide any bibliographic records whatsoever. One of them is *OECD iLibrary*, the successor to *SourceOECD*. This is a big collection comprising twenty thematic book collections.

In cases where bibliographic records are not available, some libraries create records themselves. Libraries have different attitudes towards creating records for e-books. Some libraries prefer print and e-editions to have separate records, but others like both print and e-editions to share a single record. Some mix these two approaches and have both single and separate records in the catalogues. The OCLC guidelines for cataloguing electronic resources say: 'Creating separate records for an item is preferable when both remote access electronic versions and tangible or direct access (including, but not limited to, print and other nonelectronic) versions exist. You may, however, find a single-record approach is better for your local environment.'[47]

Single records

Cataloguing departments are usually working under pressure and it is not easy to find resources to do additional work. Adding a URL to an existing record is a quick and easy way to make an electronic item available. It also brings print and e-editions together in the same records on the library OPAC, which is appreciated by library users.

However, the experience of libraries with big collections proves that this approach doesn't save time in the long run. If, for example, a number of e-books become unavailable, superseded by new editions for example, URLs have to be deleted from individual bibliographic records, and unfortunately this often has to be done manually. Depending on the workflows of individual libraries, this can mean that both bibliographic and holdings records have to be edited.

Separate records

Creating separate records for new e-books is more laborious, but enables many tasks related to administering e-books to be done in an automated way, so records do not have to be dealt with individually and manually. For libraries with hundreds of thousands of e-books in their collections, this is a significant factor.

On the other hand, separate records for print and electronic versions can clutter library OPACs with unnecessary duplicate records. This problem can, however, be solved by improved ILS software. Primo, the Ex-Libris delivery and discovery platform, identifies bibliographic records for print and e-book versions of the same edition, and displays them under one record.

Provider-neutral (P-N) records

Over the years, identical editions of digital monographs have become available from multiple providers, which resulted in many duplicate MARC records for online resources in shared bibliographic utilities and local catalogues. The solution is seen in the provider-neutral e-book record, or a single bibliographic record that can cover all equivalent manifestations of an online monograph.

Provider-Neutral E-Monograph MARC Record Guide[48] contains background information, a metadata application profile (MAP), and examples of provider-neutral e-monograph records. The P-N model was implemented in August 2009 with the recommendation that all e-monographic resources catalogued on OCLC should follow it.

P-N records are used for all instances of an online monograph, which is a huge help in instances when individual bibliographic records need to be created. However, it is still easier to have separate records for individual vendors for automatic bibliographic control purposes. The P-N approach will be really useful only if it is widely implemented by libraries and vendors.

One of the main problems related to bibliographic records is the inadequacy of integrated library systems. As Webster has noted, integrated library systems remain at the centre of library materials management.[49] They have been designed to deal with one record at a time, and don't facilitate the automated creation and checking of bibliographic records for e-books. Some improvement is seen lately in the OCLC cataloguing client, which now allows the extraction of metadata from web pages and PDF files to automatically populate bibliographic records. The OCLC cataloguing client also has the ability to work in the OCLC database, or in a local file. In the local file a global changes facility allows changes and additions to be made to a large number of records at the same time. Another very interesting feature is a macro that creates a generic provider-neutral electronic resource record from an existing print record or blank workbook record in one click. This applet was written by Donal O'Sullivan, Electronic Resources Cataloguer at the University of California, San Diego.

There are also several very useful standalone programmes, like MarcEdit, MARC Global and MARC Report, which are helpful when working with e-book records.

MarcEdit[50] is a free MARC editing tool, developed in 2000 by Terry Reese, in response to a database clean-up project on the Oregon State University's electronic catalogue. It has been continuously developed and is widely used by cataloguers. The start screen of this program can be seen in Figure 4.6.

Figure 4.6 The start screen of MarcEdit

MARCReport and MARCGlobal are programs developed by The MARC of Quality, a company that also provides cataloguing training and database services. MARCReport validates MARC records according to the latest MARC21 standards, and does cataloguing crosschecks to identify other MARC problems, such as wrong coding. It also includes a MARC editor and many integrated MARC utilities. MARCGlobal is a tool that can 'find and replace' data in MARC records. Figure 4.7 shows the MARCGlobal screen which lists the types of global changes that are possible.

These programs can be used for checking and fixing bibliographic records supplied by e-book vendors before loading them into the catalogue, and also for the automatic creation of new records. Libraries often receive large files, sometimes containing several thousand records, to be batch-loaded to the system. Such numbers make it impossible to carry out standard bibliographical control. They cannot

Figure 4.7 The start screen of MARC Global

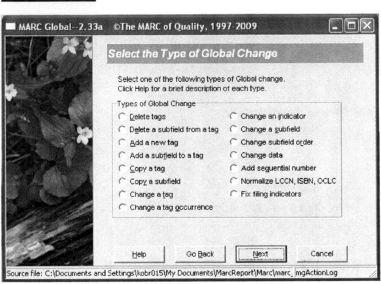

replace copy cataloguing completely, but they can find and repair mistakes in MARC tagging, coding and punctuation.

The use of MarcEdit, as well as Word and Excel, to correct and improve *netLibrary* bibliographic records has been described in great detail by Sanchez et al.[51] University of Auckland cataloguers have also been using MARC Global to clone records for e-books from existing records for print editions.

The main problems libraries experience with vendor-supplied MARC records are that not all vendors and publishers provide them, updates are not supplied when needed, and the quality varies significantly. High-quality metadata is necessary for e-book discovery in library catalogues, and for communication between different library catalogues.

MARC records may not be in use for ever. They will most likely be replaced by another type of metadata, but the need for records that comply with standards and can facilitate data exchange between different databases will remain. Libraries should campaign to encourage vendors to provide records in ways that suit library needs – to provide good-quality records, and send them in batches in a timely manner.

In March 2009, OCLC hosted a Symposium for Publishers and Librarians on Metadata.[52] This symposium brought together representatives from libraries, the publisher supply chain and organisations supporting these communities. The agenda had two items: the exploration of current models of publisher and library metadata and the consideration of new paradigms. OCLC and National Information Standards Organization (NISO) sponsored a follow-up study on metadata life cycles and workflows.[53]

The joint NISO/OCLC white paper written by Judy Luther is an excellent overview of metadata creation and transformation, including the roles played by booksellers, wholesalers and publishers. Both NISO and OCLC are of the opinion that metadata should be exchanged seamlessly between different stakeholder systems to the benefit of all. The report gives several ideas on how this can be achieved and concludes that 'in the short term, crosswalks between publisher and library systems will allow sharing of metadata among stakeholders. Long term best practices that enable translation between standards will serve all stakeholders in the industry'.[54]

De-selection

The view is often heard that one advantage of e-books is that they do not have to be weeded from library collections. However, e-books do not necessarily remain in the collection for ever; it is only that the reasons for de-selection might be different than those for print books. Based on low usage statistics, a library might decide to stop subscribing to an e-book collection, or, as is case with the *Safari* model, to swap a title that is not being used for another one that might attract more users. As with print books, e-books get replaced with new editions and libraries might prefer to remove books with superseded content. Libraries may also decide to cease collecting in a certain subject area.

The 2009 Association of Research Libraries (ARL) survey[55] found that only three ARL member libraries have a policy on deselecting e-books. However, a great number of libraries commented that de-selection of e-books was covered in their collection development policies, and many of them confirmed that they had at least some activity in this area. A small number said that they have not considered e-book de-selection, either because their collections are too small or because they intend to provide long-term access to e-books.

Interlibrary loan

Tertiary libraries are committed to providing their students and faculty with all the published books, journal articles and other texts they require. E-books are seen as having many benefits in the context of interlibrary loan (ILL) and a great potential to improve it. The nature of electronic documents makes document delivery between libraries cheaper and much more efficient. Lending a print book to another library involves costs related to processing, mailing and storage. A print book can be damaged in transfer, and if this happens, the borrowing library has to replace it. When a print book is issued to another library it is unavailable to the library's own patrons. The requester has to wait several days for the book to arrive by post. By making an e-book available to another library/libraries can avoid all the above.

However, e-books do not fit into the framework of interlibrary loan. ILL of e-books does not appeal to publishers, and Vigen and Paulson say that this is precisely because 'publishers consider them too easy to exchange'.[56]

As Woods and Ireland have noted, there are two barriers that prevent the easy sharing of e-books: technology protection measures that limit e-book use and the fact that libraries typically license e-books and do not own them.[57] Restrictive licences and digital rights management do not normally allow e-books to be part of the traditional ILL model. Licensing agreements, as well as pricing and access models, place constraints on how these collections are used. This is an issue of concern to libraries, as it prevents them using ILL as a mechanism to reach beyond the limited resources of their institutions, particularly in times when budgets are tight. According to ebrary's *Global eBook survey*, the majority of the respondents (59 per cent) said that interlibrary loan of e-books is somewhat to very important for them.[58]

The 2009 ALPSP survey found that out of 80 publishers who answered this question, just over half allowed e-book material to be used for interlibrary loan, and 16.3 per cent of respondents required that the materials are printed out prior to being interloaned. Non-profit publishers are less likely to permit interlibrary loan, but are more likely to allow it to be done entirely electronically.[59]

To ascertain the impact of e-books on interlending at the University of Auckland Library, I interviewed librarians from our Interlibrary Loans and Document Delivery department. The Library has seen an increase in ILL and document delivery activity, and the reason is that, since 2007, the complete library catalogue is represented on WorldCat. Most requests received are for journal articles and book chapters. Requests for whole books are rare in comparison. Several times a week there is a request to supply an e-book, or a chapter from an e-book. Restrictive licenses and digital rights management create very interesting situations. Sometimes a request is received for a chapter of a title for which we have both electronic and print versions. Because of the licence restrictions, or difficulties with printing and downloading, our ILL librarians have to copy the chapter from the print version. This practice is common in other libraries too.

Many authors see the pay-per-view model as the answer to problems with ILL of e-books. This model was developed by *e-Book Library (EBL)* with advice from academic libraries, e-book publishers and software developers. The model is also referred to as 'just-in-time' and 'short-term circulation', which reflects the fact that the content is borrowed only when it is needed, and only for as long as it is needed. Libraries do not have to lease or purchase content, but pay for access as determined by student and faculty use.

This model has been praised by various authors. Allen McKiel, who provided the survey analysis for *ebrary's Global eBook survey*, believes that the pay-per-view model could provide a parallel mechanism to traditional interlibrary loan.[60] Penny Garrod notes that 'short-term circulation provides a quicker, and sometimes less expensive option to interlibrary loans'.[61]

The model is still not widely accepted and a number of questions remain. It is restricted to a limited number of e-book titles offered by the vendor/publisher and pay-per-view rates can be many times higher than the cost of document delivery services operated by libraries. However, libraries with restricted budgets may find it cheaper to pay for short-term loans as opposed to purchasing e-books outright. Many e-books are purchased as part of collections, and pay-per-view would have advantages here as well. As McKiel says, 'Optimal institutional access to some collections might best be served through purchase, others through subscription, and some through pay-per-view.'[62]

The eBook Loan Service introduced by the Canada Institute for Scientific and Technical Information (CISTI), in collaboration with Ingram's *MyiLibrary*, is an interesting initiative.[63] The aim was to create a service that would modify existing technology to offer e-book loan transactions not linked to licensing models. CISTI purchased *MyiLibrary* metadata for 20,000 e-books from a variety of scholarly publishers, including Springer, Elsevier and Taylor & Francis. When they click on the e-book link in the CISTI online catalogue, clients are taken to the *MyiLibrary* site, where the loan transaction is completed. They can borrow the e-book for one month and pay by credit card. The service was launched in 2007 and is an example of the successful implementation of new models emerging in the library community about ways to improve access to scholarly literature in the digital age. However, as with the *e-Book Library* model, the eBook Loan Service model is limited to titles licensed to CISTI in the project, and to people who know that they should search the CISTI catalogue to find these titles.

Another way to overcome ILL issues and make e-books more accessible to end-users is for consortia to acquire e-book collections.[64] Consortial deals are beneficial for both libraries and their patrons. However, neither pay-per-view nor consortial deals can provide a total solution to academic libraries' efforts to support the information resource needs of their students and faculty. No single library (or consortium) will ever have everything users need in its own collection. In times when library budgets are struggling and the number of purchased print books is declining, the need for ILL and document delivery remains.

Kari Paulson and Jens Vigen observed in 2003 that 'the publishing industry has much more to gain by introducing an e-book lending model for ILL than by preserving the present situation which favours the courier and leaves the author, the publisher and the librarian out of pocket'.[65] Hopefully, the future will see some changes in this area.

Preservation

The findings of the International Data Corporation (IDC) on worldwide information growth through 2011 are fascinating. Their 2008 study[66] predicted that the digital universe will double in size every 18 months. Information created, captured or replicated in digital form in 2007 was 281 exabytes (or 281 billion gigabytes). In 2011, the amount of digital information produced is estimated to be nearly 1,800 exabytes, which means that the digital universe will be ten times the size it was in 2006 (see Figure 4.8).

The study says:

> The number of digital 'atoms' [the digital bits, or binary 1s and 0s] in the digital universe is already bigger than the number of stars in the universe. And, because the digital universe is expanding by a factor of 10 every five years, in 15 years it will surpass Avogadro's number.[67] But the size and explosive growth of the digital universe are only two of its characteristics. Like our own physical universe, it is also incredibly diverse, has hotspots, and is subject to mysterious unseen forces. It seems to have its own laws of physics.

The IDC 2008 research confirms earlier findings in the 2007 IDC white paper,[68] that approximately 70 per cent of the

Figure 4.8 Digital universe growth rate according to IDC research

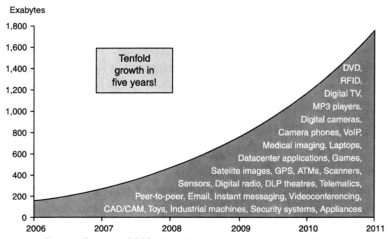

Digital Information Created, Captured, Replicated Worldwide

Source: Gantz, J.F., et al. (2008). *The Diverse and Exploding Digital Universe: An Updated Forecast of Worldwide Information Growth Through 2011.* Available from *http://www.emc.com/collateral/analyst-reports/diverse-exploding-digital-universe. pdf* (accessed 2 July 2010)

digital universe is created by individuals, but enterprises are responsible for the security, privacy, reliability, and compliance of 85 per cent of it. The study predicts that by the 2011 almost half of the digital universe will not have a permanent home.

Research and learning are increasingly supported by digital content. Particularly worrying is the fact that more and more scholarly content is 'born digital' with no print counterpart. This means that libraries are under pressure to protect access to scholarly resources, learning materials and cultural artefacts, and some commentators are saying that preservationists have the most challenging job in the field of librarianship.[69]

Today's scholarly e-books are offered mostly via the Internet and their long-term preservation is not assured.

There is no guarantee that they will be available in the future. Formats in which they are provided can become obsolete. E-book providers can go out of business. Servers on which e-books are stored can be damaged. Libraries themselves create electronic texts, often through digitisation projects whose aim is the long-term preservation of valuable collections. Formats of these e-books and platforms are equally threatened.

The International Organisation for Standardisation (ISO) has encouraged the development of standards in support of the long-term preservation of digital information. They requested the Consultative Committee for Space Data Systems (CCSDS) to coordinate the development of a reference model for an Open Archival Information System (OAIS).[70] The model provides a framework for long-term archiving and a set of terms and concepts which enable effective preservation processes.

There are a number of preservation initiatives whose goals are to minimise access risks relating to the long-term provision of digital content. Most of them are joint ventures, and include all parties involved in the production of digital texts: libraries, e-book publishers and software developers.

- LOCKSS (Lots of Copies Keep Stuff Safe) is a project run under the patronage of Stanford University. It develops and supports an open source system that allows libraries to collect, preserve and provide their readers with access to material published on the web. The system attempts to replicate the way libraries do this for material published on paper. It was originally designed for scholarly journals, but is now used to preserve all formats and genres of digital content.[71]

- CLOCKSS (Controlled LOCKSS) is a not-for-profit project run by the world's leading scholarly publishers and research libraries. The aim of it is to build a sustainable, geographically distributed dark archive which will ensure the long-term preservation of web-based scholarly publications. 'Triggered content', i.e. content no longer available from any publisher, is available free to anyone. CLOCKSS uniquely assigns this abandoned and orphaned content with a creative commons license to ensure it remains available for ever. Content is preserved on four continents: North America, Asia, Australia and Europe.[72]

■ The Digital Preservation Coalition was established in the UK in 2001 as a not-for-profit membership organisation. The aims of the Coalition are to support its members in ensuring long-term access to, and management of, their digital assets; to collaborate with UK and international partners in progressing the digital preservation and asset management agenda; and to act as a broker, and an agent of knowledge transfer amongst its membership.[73]

■ PANDORA (Preserving and Accessing Networked Documentary Resources of Australia) was established by the National Library of Australia in 1996. It now includes several Australian libraries and cultural sector organisations, and is a growing collection of Australian online publications.[74]

■ Portico is a digital preservation and electronic archiving service provided by ITHAKA, a not-for-profit organization. It was created in 2002 with the aim of providing the academic community with a sustainable digital archive of scholarly publishing. As of April 2010, 94 publishers and over 650 libraries around the world are participating in Portico. Portico preserves e-journals, e-books, and other electronic scholarly content, to a total of 14,975,138 archival units. The number of e-book titles is 33,246.[75]

Many other initiatives are under way around the world. A number of libraries run preservation programmes, including the Library of Congress,[76] the National Library of New Zealand[77] and the Koninklijke Bibliotheek, National Library of the Netherlands whose *e-depot*[78] site is considered a model for electronic deposit systems.

Library management systems developers are also working in this area. ExLibris has created Rosetta, a digital preservation product that libraries can use to save digital resources in a sustainable format, and that manages their ongoing usability. The aim is to provide libraries with the infrastructure and technology needed to preserve and facilitate permanent access to digital collections under their guardianship. Publishing companies are also conscious of the need for long-term preservation of e-books. Heather Ruland Staines provides an overview of Springer's participation in major digital preservation initiatives and explores some of the technical and legal issues that surround preservation of e-book content.[79]

The ALPSP conducted a survey in 2008 on preservation strategies among ALPSP members. The survey was sent to 240 publishers and was completed by 68. One finding was that publishers make a distinction between ensuring long-term access and long-term preservation. The majority believe that they have responsibility for long-term access and would prefer other groups and institutions to take responsibility for long-term preservation. Almost all respondents considered long-term preservation to be a critical issue, and many supported various preservation schemes. The survey revealed a wide range of concerns and an overall lack of confidence, with a high number of publishers admitting to either not trusting their current strategy, or not having any strategy at all.[80]

Another ALPSP survey done in 2009 shed further light on publishers' attitudes towards providing perpetual access to subscribed materials – an important issue for libraries in cases where they subscribe to e-book collections on the basis that 'after cancellation of a subscription, where access is maintained to the content that was actually subscribed to, on the basis that this is equivalent to keeping the print copies of subscription publications that had been received, although the subscription had been subsequently cancelled'.[81] Out of 67 publishers that answered this question, 44.8 per cent said that they provide perpetual access to e-books, 14.9 per cent of them do so online and for free, and the same percentage of publishers charge an access or maintenance fee for the service. The others provide files for local hosting, CD-ROMs or the printed books. Commercial publishers are more likely to offer perpetual access than non-profit publishers, and large and medium-sized publishers are much more likely to offer perpetual access than small publishers. The survey also found that 30.5 per cent of publishers made formal arrangements for the preservation of their e-books, 42.7 per cent had not made any plans and 26.8 per cent were planning to do so in the near future.

The continuous increase in electronic scholarly publishing raises many important issues. There is a great diversity of preservation strategies and a range of open questions relating to long-term preservation – the adequacy of formats and technical requirements, costs of preservation and the management of rights and responsibilities.

The Final Report from the Blue Ribbon Task Force on Sustainable Digital Preservation and Access, called *Sustainable Economics for a Digital Planet: Ensuring Long-term Access to Digital Information*, attempts to answer some of them. The Task Force is a collaborative project of the National Science Foundation and the Andrew W. Mellon Foundation, in partnership with the Library of Congress, the Joint Information Systems Committee of the United Kingdom, the Council on Library and Information Resources, and the National Archives and Records Administration. The report focuses on the economic challenges of preserving digital information. It states that institutions such as libraries, archives and research institutes have a critical role in convening stakeholders and sponsoring cooperation and collaboration.

The Task Force makes several recommendations about developing public–private partnerships, modifying copyright laws, raising awareness of the urgency, and ensuring technical support and training for everyone involved. The report also says that sustainable preservation strategies are not built in one attempt, nor are they static. 'A key element of a robust sustainability strategy is to anticipate the effect of these changes and take steps to minimise the risk that long-term preservation goals will be impacted by short-term disruptions in resources, incentives, and other economic factors.'[82]

Notes and references

1. Wells, A. (2008) *E-Books and Echidnas: Looking Beyond the Spines*. Paper presented at the Emerging Paradigms for Academic Library E-Book Acquisition and Use: Trends, Challenges and Opportunities. Retrieved on 2 July 2010 from *http://dspace.cityu.edu. hk/handle/2031/5166*.

2. Kyrillidou, M. and Bland, L. (eds) (2008) *ARL Statistics 2007–2008*. Washington, DC: Association of Research Libraries. Retrieved 2 July 2010 from *http://www.arl. org/bm~doc/arlstat08.pdf*.

3. Primary Research Group. (2008) *Library Use of E-books*. New York: Primary Research Group.

4. See *http://www.kuali.org/ole*.

5. *The Open Library Environment Project Final Report* (2009) Retrieved 2 July 2010 from *http://*

*oleproject.org/wp-content/uploads/2009/11/OLE_
FINAL_Report1.pdf.*

6. Anson, C. and Connell, R.R. (2009) *E-book
Collections.* Washington, DC: Association of Research
Libraries.

7. *ebrary's Global eBook Survey* (2007). Retrieved 2 July
2010 from *http://www.ebrary.com/corp/collateral/en/
Survey/ebrary_eBook_survey_2007.pdf*

8. Ibid.

9. Cleary, C. (2008) 'CEIRC questionnaire on e-book
purchasing, June 2007', *Access,* 65(June). Retrieved
2 July 2010 from *http://www.aardvarknet.info/access/
number65/monthnews.cfm?monthnews=01.*

10. Anson, C. and Connell, R.R. (2009) *E-book Collections.*
Washington, DC: Association of Research Libraries.

11. Levine-Clark, M. (2007) 'Electronic books and the
approval plan: can they work together?', *Against the
Grain,* 19(2).

12. Dunham, B. and Davis, T.L. (2009) 'Literature of
acquisitions in review, 2004–7', *Library Resources &
Technical Services,* 53(4).

13. Anson, C. and Connell, R.R. (2009) *E-book Collections.*
Washington, DC: Association of Research Libraries.

14. Ibid.

15. See *http://infomotions.com/blog/tag/vufind/.*

16. See *http://www.lib.uwaterloo.ca/newsatlib/100126/primo.
html.*

17. See *http://www.oclc.org/worldcatlocal/overview/metase
arch/.*

18. Dinkelman, A. and Stacy-Bates, K. (2007) 'Accessing
e-Books through academic library web sites', *College
and Research Libraries,* 68(1).

19. By connecting to Google Scholar, Google Books and
Scirus via EZproxy, the University of Auckland users

have access to the subscription-only material to which the University Library subscribes.

20. E-Book Focus Group (2008) *Ex Libris/ELUNA/ IGeLU Recommendations and Requirements for E-Book Functionality.* Retrieved 2 July 2010 from *http://documents.el-una.org/186/.*

21. *ebrary's Global eBook Survey* (2007). Retrieved 2 July 2010 from *http://www.ebrary.com/corp/collateral/en/ Survey/ebrary_eBook_survey_2007.pdf.*

22. See *http://www.ebook88.com/devices.html.*

23. See *http://ebook-reader-review.toptenreviews.com/.*

24. See *http://ereaderresource.com.*

25. Primary Research Group (2008) *Library Use of E-books.* New York: Primary Research Group.

26. Rodzvilla, J. (2009) 'The portable e-book: issues with e-book reading devices in the library', *Serials: The Journal for the Serials Community,* 22(3, Supplement 1).

27. D'Agostino, D. (7 January 2010) 'The strange case of academic libraries and e-books nobody reads', *TeleRead: Bring the E-Books Home.* Retrieved 2 July 2010 from *http://www.teleread.org/2010/01/07/the-strange-case-of-academic-libraries-and-e-books-nobody-reads/.*

28. Ibid.

29. For more information about this project see *http://www. libraries.psu.edu/psul/lls/sony_reader.html.*

30. Lee, H. (28 September 2009) 'Kindles yet to woo University users', *The Daily Princetonian.* Retrieved 2 July 2010 from *http://www.dailyprincetonian.com/2009 /09/28/23918/.*

31. Chen, B.X. (5 April 2010) 'Colleges dream of paperless, iPad-centric education', *Wired.* Retrieved 2 July 2010 from *http://www.wired.com/gadgetlab/2010/04/ipad-text books/.*

32. Korn, M. (16 April 2010) 'Apple's IPad rejected by some colleges, for now', *The Wall Street Journal Digital Network*. Retrieved 2 July 2010 from *http://online.wsj.com/article/BT-CO-20100416-712117.html.*

33. See *http://www.coursesmart.com/go/ipad/index.html.*

34. See *http://www.youtube.com/watch?v=kSjXO7Odh9E.*

35. Paul, I. (3 April 2010) 'Interactive textbooks headed to iPad, report says', *PCWorld Blog*. Retrieved 2 July 2020 from *http://www.pcworld.com/article/188427/interactive_textbooks_headed_to_ipad_report_says.html.*

36. Solomons, T. (2004) *Beam Me Up! Supporting PDAs (Personal Digital Assistants) in Medical Libraries: New Technology, or Just Another Format?* Paper presented at the VALA conference. Retrieved 2 July 2010 from *http://www.vala.org.au/vala2004/2004pdfs/57Solom.PDF.*

37. Zheng, L. and Tan, S. (2009) *E-books in China: Develop and Use.* Paper presented at the IFLA Conference. Retrieved 2 July 2010 from *http://www.ifla.org/files/hq/papers/ifla75/212-zheng-en.pdf.*

38. Ally, M. (ed) (2009) *Mobile Learning: Transforming the Delivery of Education and Training.* Retrieved 2 July 2010 from *http://www.aupress.ca/books/120155/ebook/99Z_Mohamed_Ally_2009-Mobile Learning.pdf.*

39. Cox, J. and Cox, L. (2010) *Scholarly Book Publishing Practice: An ALPSP Survey of Academic Book Publishers' Policies and Practices, First Survey, 2009.* Shoreham-by-Sea: Association of Learned and Professional Society Publishers.

40. Mason, D. (2001) 'Cataloguing for libraries in a digital world', in B. Cope and D. Mason (eds), *Digital Book Production and Supply Chain Management.* Altona, Vic.: Common Ground Publishing.

41. Ibid.

42. JISC (2003) *Promoting the Uptake of E-Books in Higher and Further Education: Joint Information Systems Committee Report*. Retrieved 2 July 2010 from *http://www.jisc.ac.uk/uploaded_documents/PromotingeBooksReportB.pdf*.

43. Dillon, D. (2001) 'E-books: the University of Texas experience, part 1', *Library Hi Tech*, 19(2).

44. Connaway, L. and Snyder, C. (2005) 'Transaction log analysis of electronic (eBook) usage', *Against the Grain*, 17(1).

45. Rossmann, D., Foster, A. and Babbitt, E.P. (2009) 'E-book MARC records: do they make the mark?', *Serials: The Journal for the Serials Community*, 22(3).

46. *eBooks – The End User Perspective* (2009). Retrieved 2 July 2010 from *http://www.springer.com/cda/content/document/cda_downloaddocument/eBooks+-+the+End+User+Experience?SGWID=0-0-45-608298-0*.

47. Weitz, J. (2006) *Cataloging Electronic Resources: OCLC-MARC Coding Guidelines*. Retrieved 2 July 2010 from *http://www.oclc.org/us/en/support/documentation/worldcat/cataloging/electronicresources/*.

48. Culbertson, B., Mandelstam, Y. and Prager, G. (2009) *Provider-Neutral E-Monograph MARC Record Guide*. Retrieved 2 July 2010 from *http://www.loc.gov/catdir/pcc/bibco/PN-Guide.pdf*.

49. Webster, P.M. (2008) *Managing Electronic Resources: New and Changing Roles for Libraries*. Oxford: Chandos.

50. Additional information about MarcEdit can be found at *http://people.oregonstate.edu/~reeset/marcedit/html/index.php*.

51. Sanchez, E., Fatout, L., Howser, A. and Vance, C. (2006) 'Cleanup of Netlibrary cataloging records: a methodical front-end process', *Technical Services Quarterly*, 23(4).

52. See *www.oclc.org/publisher-symposium/*.

53. Register, R. (2009) 'OCLC Symposium for Publishers and Librarians on Metadata', *Information Standards Quarterly*, 21(2). Retrieved 2 July 2010 from *http:// www.oclc.org/publisher-symposium/resources/OCLC_ Symposium_article.pdf*.

54. Luther, J. (2009) *Streamlining Book Metadata Workflow*. Retrieved 2 July 2010 from *http://www. niso.org/publications/white_papers/Streamline BookMetadataWorkflowWhitePaper.pdf*.

55. Anson, C. and Connell, R.R. (2009) *E-book Collections*. Washington, DC: Association of Research Libraries.

56. Vigen, J. and Paulson, K. (2003) *E-books and Interlibrary Loan: An Academic Centric Model for Lending*. Paper presented at the 8th Interlending and Document Supply Conference. Retrieved 2 July 2010 from *www.nla.gov. au/ilds/abstracts/ebooksand.htm*.

57. Woods, B. and Ireland, M. (2008) 'eBook loans: an e-twist on a classic interlending service', *Interlending and Document Supply*, 36(2). Retrieved 2 July 2010 from *www.emeraldinsight.com/10.1108/02641610810878585*.

58. *ebrary's Global eBook Survey* (2007) Retrieved 2 July 2010 from *http://www.ebrary.com/corp/collateral/en/ Survey/ebrary_eBook_survey_2007.pdf*.

59. Cox, J. and Cox, L. (2010) *Scholarly Book Publishing Practice: An ALPSP Survey of Academic Book Publishers' Policies and Practices, First Survey, 2009*. Shoreham-by-Sea: Association of Learned and Professional Society Publishers.

60. *ebrary's Global eBook Survey* (2007) Retrieved 2 July 2010 from *http://www.ebrary.com/corp/collateral/en/ Survey/ebrary_eBook_survey_2007.pdf*.

61. Garrod, P. (2004) 'E-books: are they the interlibrary lending model of the future?', *Interlending and*

Document Supply, 32(4). Retrieved from *www.emeraldinsight.com/10.1108/02641610410567971*

62. *ebrary's Global eBook Survey* (2007). Retrieved from *http://www.ebrary.com/corp/collateral/en/Survey/ebrary_eBook_survey_2007.pdf*

63. Woods, B. and Ireland, M. (2008) 'eBook loans: an e-twist on a classic interlending service', *Interlending and Document Supply,* 36(2). Retrieved 2 July 2010 from *www.emeraldinsight.com/10.1108/02641610810878585.*

64. Garrod, P. (2004) 'E-books: are they the interlibrary lending model of the future?', *Interlending and Document Supply,* 32(4). Retrieved 2 July 2010 from *www.emeraldinsight.com/10.1108/02641610410567971.*

65. Vigen, J. and Paulson, K. (2003) *E-books and Interlibrary Loan: An Academic Centric Model for Lending.* Paper presented at the 8th Interlending and Document Supply Conference. Retrieved 2 July 2010 from *www.nla.gov.au/ilds/abstracts/ebooksand.htm.*

66. Gantz, J.F. et al. (2008) *The Diverse and Exploding Digital Universe: An Updated Forecast of Worldwide Information Growth Through 2011.* Retrieved 2 July 2010 from *http://www.emc.com/collateral/analyst-reports/diverse-exploding-digital-universe.pdf.*

67. The number of atoms or molecules in one mole of a substance, equal to 6.023×10^{23} (from *Oxford Dictionary of English* (2005) Oxford: Oxford University Press).

68. Gantz, J.F. et al. (2007) *The Expanding Digital Universe: A Forecast of Worldwide Information Growth Through 2010.* Retrieved 2 July 2010 from *http://www.emc.com/collateral/analyst-reports/expanding-digital-idc-white-paper.pdf.*

69. Morgan, E.L. (4 April 2010) 'Preservationists have the most challenging job', *Mini-Musings.* Retrieved 2 July

2010 from *http://infomotions.com/blog/2010/01/ preservationists-have-the-most-challenging-job/*.

70. Consultative Committee for Space Data Systems (2002) *Reference Model for an Open Archival Information System (OAIS)*. Washington, DC: CCSDS Secretariat.

71. See *http://lockss.stanford.edu/lockss/Home*.

72. See *http://www.clockss.org/clockss/Home*.

73. See *http://www.dpconline.org/about/index.html*.

74. See *http://pandora.nla.gov.au*.

75. See *http://www.portico.org/digital-preservation/*.

76. See *http://www.digitalpreservation.gov*.

77. See *http://www.natlib.govt.nz/about-us/current-initiatives/ ndha*.

78. See *http://www.kb.nl/hrd/dd/index-en.html*.

79. Staines, H.R. (2009) 'Springer's eBook Preservation Strategy', *Against the Grain*, 21(1).

80. Durrant, S. (2008) *Long-Term Preservation: Results from a Survey Investigating Preservation Strategies Amongst ALPSP Publisher Members*. Retrieved 2 July 2010 from *http://www.alpsp.org/ngen_public/article. asp?id=200&did=47&aid=27137&st=&oaid=-1*.

81. Cox, J. and Cox, L. (2010) *Scholarly Book Publishing Practice: An ALPSP survey of Academic Book Publisher's Policies and Practices, First Survey, 2009*. Shoreham-by-Sea: Association of Learned and Professional Society Publishers.

82. Blue Ribbon Task Force on Sustainable Digital Preservation and Access (2010) *Sustainable Economics for a Digital Planet: Ensuring Long-term Access to Digital Information*. Retrieved 2 July 2010 from *http:// brtf.sdsc.edu/biblio/BRTF_Final_Report.pdf*.

5

Connecting with users

Several years ago I did a little 'e-book test' on my son and his friends. It was in 2004 when I was doing research on the use of e-books at the University of Auckland Library. My son was already a few months into his first year at the university, and out of curiosity I asked him and his freshmen friends what they knew about e-books. The answer was a big surprise to me. These young people belong to a generation which does not remember the time before computers and the Internet. They have all had computers at home and at school from an early age, and know all about the latest IT developments. All of them were even taking at least one computer-related paper in their first semester. Yet they knew nothing about the Library's e-book collections. The concept of electronic texts as such was familiar, they had clear ideas of what an e-book might be, they used electronic articles, and had maybe even read a few free e-books available on the Internet, but they did not know that any e-book collections existed in the Library, and, consequently, they had never used any of them.

I am mentioning this story only as an illustration that nothing is obvious and as proof that, if libraries would like a particular type of material to be used, they have to ensure users know that it exists in library collections.

Some authors predict that e-books will be widely adopted within the next few years. The *2010 Horizon Report* says that electronic books are quickly reaching the point where their advantages over printed books are compelling, and gives two to three years as the time to adoption.[1] Mark Nelson also predicts that e-books will soon overtake printed books on campuses.[2] But even if e-books have become firmly established in the private sector, the question of students' perception of libraries will remain. At what point will it be natural for them to assume that libraries have e-books too? The other question is: at what point will lecturers start listing more e-books in their reading lists?

Bringing e-books to users

Mark Nelson points out that there are two types of barriers to e-book acceptance – technical and cultural.[3] Libraries are not in a position to make much difference with regard to technical barriers, but they have put a great deal of effort into breaking cultural barriers. Promotion of awareness and use of e-books has been generally recognised as necessary to ensure the use of e-books on campuses. Libraries spend a significant amount of their budgets on e-books, and it is important for them to ensure a return on their investments in e-book collections.

E-book collections should be promoted to all potential users – students, teachers and library staff. Subject librarians need to be aware of potential uses in the academic environment and of the advantages e-books offer in their particular disciplines, so they can pass on that knowledge to faculty and students. E-books are available in a variety of models and platforms and librarians have to learn about these to be able to use them proficiently. They need initial instruction when new platforms are purchased, but also information about subsequent changes and improvements. Likewise, teaching staff should have a thorough knowledge of e-books as a medium, as well as of collections available in the libraries of their universities, so that they can recommend e-books as part of their courses. Students should be aware of available e-book collections, and know how to make full use of special features such as notes and bookmarking.

In the 2008 Springer survey of end-user perspectives, respondents identified lack of awareness of e-book resources available through their libraries as the primary obstacle to e-book usage. 'Fortunately, libraries have the power to remove this obstacle by improving the ease of finding eBooks and educating library users about the availability of eBooks as part of library collections.'[4]

Because people have different learning preferences (reading manuals, asking friends, trial and error, attending courses) it is important to offer a range of options. For this reason libraries use a variety of methods to promote e-book collections and instruct users. These include simple announcements on the front pages of library websites, articles in newsletters and library blogs, as well as detailed instructions on particular collections.

Many academic libraries create dedicated e-book pages as part of their websites. In a study carried out by Dinkelman and Stacy-Bates, which examined Association of Research Libraries (ARL) websites, 62 (56 per cent) of the 111 libraries included a page focusing entirely on e-books.[5]

At the University of Auckland Library the e-book page (Figure 5.1)[6] serves as a general gateway to e-books. One item on this page is a canned catalogue search that will find only e-books. The page also lists the main e-book databases with brief descriptions of each of them. The page links to a *Guide to Finding & Using E-books*,[7] and an e-book course handout, *How to Search & Use E-books*.[8] (I should note here that a complete redesign of the Library web pages is scheduled for 2010, and the e-book page will be part of this.)

Figure 5.1 The University of Auckland Library e-book page

The Electronic Resources Academic Library Link (ERALL) consortium of eight Hong Kong university libraries has developed a video about the e-books they have purchased which explains which collections are available and how to use them.[9] Library users at the University of Aberdeen library can find a variety of guides on how to access electronic resources, including vodcasts – video-style recordings (screencasts) – where users see a step-by-step guide on their computer monitors, accompanied by a spoken commentary.[10]

The Texas A&M University Libraries and a group of American Advertising Federation (AAF) undergraduate students undertook a collaborative project to develop a marketing campaign to advertise the availability of 30,000 *netLibrary* e-books. The campaign was very successful and approximately 200 new user accounts were created as a direct result, and 3,800 e-books were used within the first two weeks. The material developed for the initial promotion (screensaver ads and posters) was later used for continuing promotion of the *netLibrary* e-books. As McGeachin and Ramirez concluded, 'students benefited from having an ad campaign to include in their personal portfolios and the Libraries gained a creative and undergraduate student-focused advertising campaign'.[11]

E-book courses are another popular means of raising awareness and promoting the use of e-books among students and staff. They help students understand the nature of e-books, build an appreciation of the advantages and disadvantages of the medium and familiarise them with free and commercially-produced e-books. The University of Auckland e-book course attracts large numbers of students every year. Because of the high demand, more course sessions have been scheduled for 2010 and more seats have been made available in each session.

In a 2009 Association of Research Libraries (ARL) survey, member libraries were asked about the methods they use to educate users. The survey shows that the majority of libraries have some kind of education activity:

> To promote e-books to patrons, 48 per cent of the respondents have featured e-books in their newsletters. Others have news announcements, new title lists, or blogs that highlight new e-book acquisitions. Comments indicate that e-book education is part of bibliographer outreach activities and regular reference interviews. Others comment that e-books tend to be found regardless of library efforts.[12]

The survey also reported that libraries put a significant amount of effort into educating their own staff, with 66 per cent of responding libraries using some method to raise awareness among library staff. Educational activities undertaken at ARL member libraries are shown in Figure 5.2.

Figure 5.2	The variety of educational activities at ARL member libraries

Instruction sessions discuss e-books	56	90%
Online/print research guides identify subject appropriate e-books	49	79%
Periodic new title alerts include e-books	34	55%
Library newsletter includes articles about e-books	30	48%
Blog highlights new e-book acquisitions	27	44%
Promotional printed material	14	23%
Web tutorials describe how to find and use e-books	9	15%
Other method	11	18%

The importance of library web promotions is repeatedly confirmed; for example, in the survey conducted by the Hong Kong Institute of Education, whose e-book collections comprise more than 30,000 titles, some purchased via consortia, and some directly from vendors. The survey was carried out in 2008 and included staff, students and external members. It showed that the majority of users (61 per cent) learn about e-books from the library website, and many fewer via recommendations by professors (21 per cent) and classmates (4.5 per cent). There were also a number of students (12.5 per cent) who had never heard about e-books at all.

What users say

A number of surveys have been conducted on the information-seeking behaviour of students and faculties, and their use of electronic material. Several have been mentioned already, but in this section I will compare data from five key studies in more detail, to highlight different aspects of e-book use.

- A survey on e-book usage at the University of Denver Penrose Library (the **Denver** survey) was conducted in 2005. It was completed by 2,067 respondents, out of whom 30.1 per cent were undergraduates, 39.1 per cent graduate students, 12.5 per cent faculty members, and 11.8 per cent staff. Results were compiled by Michael Levine-Clark.[13]

- The **SuperBook** study, conducted in 2006, was funded by Wiley, Emerald and CIBER. This survey included nearly two thousand students and faculty members at the University College, London, and about three thousand selected e-texts published by Oxford Scholarship Online, Wiley Interscience and Taylor & Francis. Results were compiled by Ian Rowlands, David Nicholas, Hamid R. Jamali and Paul Huntington and published in 2007.[14]

- A **Springer** survey of end-user perspectives of e-books was conducted in 2008. It included users from five university libraries in different parts of the world.[15] It followed a 2007 Springer survey on librarians at six institutions and their views on e-book adoption and benefits.[16]

- An *ebrary* survey on students' usage, needs and perceptions with regard to e-books (*ebrary* **Student**) was done in 2008. A total of 6,492 students completed the survey, representing nearly 400 individual institutions, from approximately 75 countries.[17]

- The **JISC** national e-books observatory project involved seven publishers, two e-book aggregators and 127 United Kingdom universities.[18] A number of surveys and analyses were done as part of it. The 2008 user survey[19] was completed by 23,445 people, and the 2009 survey by 28,709 people. A report on both surveys was published in 2009.[20] The final report on the project[21] was also published in 2009. It includes data from user surveys, deep log analysis[22] of the MyiLibrary platform (from September

2007 to December 2008), focus group reports and print and circulation data reports.[23]

All these surveys have focused on users in academic environments, but they did not have the same approach. Some addressed only one type of user, for example students, while others included all types. Some questions were the same, or similar, others were completely different and responses cannot be compared. However, taken together, they do shed some light on user attitudes.

User awareness of e-books

Denver – 59.1 per cent of all respondents were aware of e-books. Undergraduate students were more aware than other types of users, 71.1 per cent of them were aware of e-books, compared with 56 per cent of graduates and 52.9 per cent of faculty members. Michael Levine-Clark explains this by the fact that undergraduates have grown up with computer technology.

SuperBook – 69 per cent of users were aware that their library provided e-books. The survey found that postgraduate (41 per cent) and undergraduate students (34 per cent) were much more aware than academic (24 per cent) and research staff (21 per cent). Engineering sciences (41 per cent) and social and historical sciences (38 per cent) were the most e-book aware, while life sciences (22 per cent) and mathematical and physical sciences (20 per cent) were the least. The survey did not show any significant differences between full- and part-timers, or that e-book use correlates with the use of print library collections.

Springer – Between 52 per cent and 84 per cent of users at each institution participating in the survey knew that their libraries provided e-books, and between 58 per cent and 80 per cent of all participants had used e-books at least once.

ebrary **Student** – More than half of the 6,492 respondents (3,507) rated their awareness of the e-books provided by their college or university library as good, almost one quarter said fair (1,663), 926 said excellent and 396 students said poor. When asked if their library had any e-books, 606 respondents said no, and 2,173 (over 33 per cent) said they did not know if their libraries had any e-books.

JISC – The 2008 and 2009 surveys both focused on general exposure to e-books and confirmed that the university population has already been highly exposed to e-books. There has been an increase in e-book usage, from 60.1 per cent of students and teachers using e-books in 2008 to 64.6 per cent in 2009. The study also found that usage varies according to gender, age, job, full or part-time status, time of day, location, type of institution and nationality.

Sources of e-books

Denver – 1,215 respondents indicated the means by which they learned about the university's provision of electronic books: 39.3 per cent said that they learned about e-books from the library catalogue, 26.7 per cent from a professor, 15.6 per cent from a librarian, 14 per cent from the library home page, and 4.4 per cent from a friend.

SuperBook – 61 per cent of all users source e-books themselves, independently of their libraries, and 35 per cent obtain e-books from library collections. Rowlands et al. conclude that 'libraries are very much the preferred source for e-books related to work or study but for their leisure reading users generally tend to find other sources'.

The study also found that websites and library catalogues were more effective awareness-raising channels for men, and staff briefings and course tutors for women. Course tutors play a vital role, with 68 per cent of undergraduates saying that they found out about library provision this way.

The survey also suggests 'that staff would very much welcome a user guide posted on the library website, that undergraduates would benefit enormously from making sure that e-books are included and signposted on reading lists, and that graduate students are able to access a printed information guide in the library'.

Springer – Users have different starting points for e-book searching in different institutions. At the University of Muenster and CWI Amsterdam, users preferred to start their searches using general search engines like Google, while at the University of Turku and the University of Illinois, users preferred library catalogues.

ebrary **Student** – 77 per cent or 2,370 respondents said they accessed e-books through the library website, while 59 per cent or 1,791 respondents said their starting point was the library catalogue, 55 per cent or 1,683 find e-books through Google and other search engines, and only 12 per cent or 363 students indicated starting at the vendor website.

Many students said that librarians introduced them to e-books (50 per cent, or 1,533 students), but library catalogues, library websites, instructors and Google were also selected by more than 40 per cent of students.

JISC – The 2009 survey showed that 51.9 per cent of students and teachers source their e-books mostly from university libraries. 38.4 per cent obtained them on the open web, and only 3.8 per cent purchased their e-books. The study also confirmed that links from library websites and catalogue records are essential for finding e-books. According to this survey, federated searches are more confusing than useful as a discovery tool. The survey also showed that nearly half the teaching staff had e-books on reading lists, with the number increasing from 43.9 per cent in 2008 to 49.4 per cent in 2009.

Frequency of use

Denver – Of the 1,116 respondents, 27.7 per cent said that they had used e-books only once, 62 per cent occasionally, and 10.3 per cent frequently. The results vary slightly among types of users, with faculty using them the most, despite their lower awareness compared to other user groups.

SuperBook – The study used a predictive model to indicate whether or not someone is likely to be an e-book user, based on their responses to other questions in the survey. The odds ratios in this model show that current users of e-books are three times as likely to be already aware of university's e-book offerings, one and a half times more likely to be male, and about 13 per cent more likely to be less than wholly satisfied with printed book collections.

Springer – Frequency of e-book usage varied from institution to institution. Most users indicated that they access e-books on a weekly or monthly basis. As key reasons for not using e-books more often, users mentioned the difficulty of reading books on screen and a preference for traditional print books.

ebrary Student – 49 per cent of respondents said that they had never used the e-books provided by their libraries. Out of the 51 per cent of respondents who had used e-books, 1,842 said they used them for less than one hour per week, 1,042 said 1 to 5 hours per week, 313 said 5 to 10 hours per week, and only 123 said more than 10 hours per week.

The huge proportion of students who have never used e-books is not surprising, considering that almost the same proportion were not aware of e-books in their libraries. But nearly half of the students who reported that they never used e-books indicated that they preferred print books. Many said that e-books are too difficult to read, too difficult to access remotely, and too difficult to use. Seven per cent of students said that they did not use e-books because e-books were not available in subject areas relevant to their courses. Some students indicated that their instructor requested them not to use e-books (53 respondents) or that they did not have access to a computer or the Internet (39 respondents).

JISC – Nearly 50 per cent of users used one or two titles per month, less than 30 per cent three to five titles per month, and about 15 per cent used more than five titles per month. Use of e-books varied throughout the year, and was closely related to the teaching cycle. Some 63 per cent of e-books were accessed on campus, 31 per cent off campus, and 6 per cent from overseas. The busiest time of the day was between 8 a.m. and 2 p.m.

Purpose of reading e-books

Denver – Reasons for preferring e-books were: electronic books allow for easier searching of the text (661 responses, or 55.4 per cent); working from home makes it difficult to get to the library (505 responses, or 42.3 per cent); and no print version of the book was available (482 responses, or 40.4 per cent). Michael Levine-Clark concluded that these answers show that respondents value the convenience of not having to go to the library and not having to wait for a print volume, as well as the ability to search within the text. He also says that users prefer electronic books for certain types of reading and, by implication, may prefer print for others.

SuperBook – 14 per cent of respondents used e-books for leisure, 15 per cent for both leisure and study, and 71 per cent for study, of the latter 59.9 per cent of them used textbooks, 52.4 per cent reference books, and 46 per cent reference monographs. It was noticeable that part-timers (both staff and students) used e-books to support their leisure activities somewhat more than full-timers did.

Springer – The survey found that the main use of e-books was for research and study, with teaching and leisure far behind. Type of e-book used varied by institution. Users at the University of Illinois at Urbana-Champaign and Muenster most often used reference works while users at the JRD Tata Memorial Library, Bangalore, accessed textbooks most often. At the University of Turku both reference works and textbooks were used, while at the Centre for Mathematics and Computer Science, Amsterdam, conference proceedings were the most often-used type of e-book.

ebrary **Student** – The survey included a range of questions on what types of resources students were using and for what purpose. The study found that for research and class assignments students almost equally use Google and other search engines (2,593 of 3,208 respondents), e-books (2,517) and print books (2,478). E-reference books, print textbooks and e-journals showed the highest usage. For personal use students prefer Google and other search engines (2,501), Wikipedia (2,320), and social web applications (2,105). Print books, magazines and newspapers were also highly used, and 1,049 students said that they used e-books for leisure reading.

E-books were considered as the second most trustworthy source for research and class assignments, after print books and before print textbooks. Asked to determine how they knew if a source was trustworthy, most students said their instructor recommended it (2,718 students) or it is published by a well-known publisher (2,250). They also said it was trustworthy because it was available through the library, or a librarian recommended it (2,145). Students also showed a high regard for peer recommendations (999). Only 454 students trusted books found through Google and other search engines.

JISC – Over 90 per cent of students and teachers said that their reason for consulting e-books was for work or study. Students rated their dependence on different information resources as follows (on a scale from 1 to 5 where 5 is most dependent): open web 3.31, lecture notes 3.06, library e-resources (including e-books) 3.03, own books 2.99, library print resources 2.92, online course materials 2.84.

Screen reading behaviour (time spent per page)

Denver – Of the 1,148 respondents, 56.5 per cent read a chapter or article within a book, 36.4 per cent read a single entry or a few pages within a book, and only 7.1 per cent read the entire book. Faculty members were more inclined to read the whole book (9.6 per cent, compared to 3 per cent of undergraduate and 7.5 per cent of graduate students), and to read a few pages within a book (42.5 per cent, compared to 37.7 per cent of undergraduate and 34.2 per cent of graduate students). Students, on the other hand, more often read only a chapter or an article (59.3 per cent of undergraduates, 58.3 per cent of graduate students, compared to 47.9 per cent of faculty members).

Springer – Users skim quickly through a variety of digital resources looking for specific pieces of information, rather than engage in extended reading sessions. The study sees e-books as a resource for finding answers to research questions, and concludes that e-books 'have the potential to stimulate new forms of book content usage and will require libraries to think differently about how to accommodate the needs of users as their eBook collections grow'.

ebrary Student – Did not ask this question specifically, but the fact that about half the students who use e-books said they used them for less than one hour per week indicates that they do not spend much time reading, and that they do not read whole books.

JISC – Over 70 per cent of online reading sessions were over 11 minutes long and 85 per cent of readers spent less than a minute viewing each e-book page. Only 5.5 per cent of students and 7.1 per cent of teachers in JISC disciplines[24] said that they read the whole book, 20 per cent of students and 14.3 per cent of teachers read several whole chapters, and 53.5 per cent of students and 58.6 per cent of teachers dipped in and out of several chapters. The JISC conclusion is that 'currently the use of e-books mostly satisfies the need for brief information and rapid fact extraction'. Cutting and pasting was common. Users preferred to print out sections to read and take notes on paper.

Reading format preference

Denver – A small majority read their e-books online, whether on a computer screen (45.5 per cent) or on a PDA (5.2 per cent). 26.2 per cent of respondents read e-book content from a printed copy, and 23.2 per cent indicated that it depends on the situation.

SuperBook – 48 per cent of respondents preferred reading from the screen, 13 per cent preferred to print and read from paper, and 39 per cent said that it varies. The survey did not indicate why and under what circumstances. Rowlands et al. noted that 'there is a strong tendency for users to read leisure materials from a computer screen but print out the contents of work or study-based materials'.

JISC – Over 60 per cent of users (both students and teaching staff) read e-books from the screen, rather than from paper. As reasons for this JISC lists 'speed, pragmatism and problems associated with printing and downloading'.

Print vs. electronic format

Denver – All groups of users preferred print over e-books: 16.6 per cent of respondents to this question indicated that they would always use print books; 44.1 per cent said that they would usually choose print but sometimes electronic; 19.4 per cent stated that they would usually opt for electronic but would sometimes choose print; 2.1 per cent would always use electronic; and 16.9 per cent felt it would depend on the situation. However, when reading e-books, most respondents do not print out e-book content, with undergraduates being much more likely than graduate students or faculty members to print a copy of the text, and less likely to read the text online.

SuperBook – This study found that e-books compare very unfavourably with print titles for perceived ease of reading.

ebrary **Student** – This study shows that students prefer electronic material: 51 per cent (1,566) of students would often or very often choose an e-book over a print book, 32 per cent (974) sometimes and 17 per cent (527) rarely or never.

JISC – Print is still the preferred format. The reasons for this are the familiarity with print format, the fact that print facilitates greater concentration, that it is easier to scan and browse, and easier for note making, annotating and highlighting.

Importance of e-book features

SuperBook – The most valued advantages of e-books revolve around convenience: ease of making copies, perceived up-to-dateness, space-saving, and 24/7 availability. The study finds that men tend to rate e-book features and functionality much more highly than women.

Springer – The benefits of e-books cluster around convenience and information access. Users valued the ability to access e-books anytime and anywhere, and appreciated fast and easy access and full-text searching. Almost all respondents said that e-books were useful, with between 79 per cent and 92 per cent of users at each institution stating that they would like to use more e-books.

ebrary **Student** – In this study the most valued characteristic of e-books was that they were environmentally friendly. More than half of the respondents also appreciated access anytime, anywhere, full-text searching and the ease of sharing and storing. The primary advantage of print books was ease of reading. Print is the format of choice for note taking and highlighting for around 40 per cent of the students. A third (33 per cent) of the respondents valued print collections for having a wide selection of titles.

JISC – Users selected online access and full-text searching as the biggest advantages of e-books. Another important advantage moment was that e-books could be a great solution for high-demand items, particularly for distance and part-time students.

What would increase e-book usage?

ebrary **Student** – More titles available in key subjects, fewer restrictions on printing and copying, and more current titles.

JISC – Users want more course-related material, more interactivity within the e-book, unlimited concurrent access, the ability to print out more than one page at a time and aggressive DRM restrictions to be lifted. They would also like to be aware of what is available (via better promotion of e-books) and more training in how to access and use e-books.

Comments

Between 50 and 80 per cent of users in each survey said they were aware of e-books. This means that a huge percentage of users, up to 50 per cent in some cases, were not aware that their libraries provided any e-books. This certainly lowers the chances of them utilising e-book collections and highlights the importance of e-book promotion.

Users in these five surveys do not differ much in their appreciation of e-books. Both advantages and disadvantages revolve around convenience of use. In other words, they appreciate all the characteristics of e-books that enhance convenience – like access anytime, anywhere, and full-text searching – and dislike limitations on access and printing.

E-books from library collections are mostly used for research and study, and much less often for leisure. This highlights the importance of having relevant titles, including textbooks, in e-book collections.

The studies show that students do not spend much time reading e-books. Instead they dip in and out, searching for the information they need. Users prefer reading print, but are happy to read smaller chunks of text on screen. The studies indicate that students make printouts for more detailed reading.

All the surveys show that libraries are an important source of e-books for study and research. Libraries also have an important role in educating users about the availability of e-books.

Springer's comment is interesting:

Clearly, even if users do not realise their library contains eBook offerings, they are encountering eBooks in their online research through sources like Google Book Search. Libraries have the opportunity to position themselves as a central, convenient source of extensive eBook content for users who would otherwise turn to the Internet for their eBook searches.

A number of other smaller studies support the findings of the five examined above. Further study carried out at the University of Denver's Penrose Library in 2006 focused specifically on undergraduate use of e-books. The authors interviewed 15 students in three disciplines (economics, literature, and nursing). They observed search behaviour closely to gather information on the types of e-books used, and noted that students browsed or scanned the content, rather than reading it entirely.[25]

A 2007 study at the University of Maryland, Eastern Shore, shows that the majority of the students who responded prefer paper-based books to e-books. The authors concluded that e-books may be 'a hard sell in higher education'.[26]

A 2004 study at the College of Mount St Joseph's Archbishop Alter Library in Cincinnati, Ohio, examined the e-book usage of 105 students in four core undergraduate courses. Students' feelings about using e-books were mixed, with students indicating that they would use e-books, but with 66 per cent of them preferring traditional print books. The study concludes that print books and e-books appeal to different learning styles.[27]

A 2007 Arizona State University focus group study of six faculty members, to ascertain their perceptions and use of e-books in relation to research and teaching, found that although their experiences with e-books had not been positive, most agreed that e-books would be a very viable and useful alternative, if issues with reliability and accessibility, lack of manipulability and the steep learning curve of the various interfaces were resolved.[28]

An interesting study on the information behaviour of the researcher of the future was commissioned by the British Library and JISC in 2007. The aim of this study was to test whether there is any evidence to suggest that modern young people, i.e. the Google generation, are different from earlier generations. The study looked at a number of earlier studies done in the field, and included users of all ages. This study was not restricted to e-books, but e-books are part of the digital information milieu, and the findings of the study are also relevant for e-books. The study concluded that the strategic implications of the shift from physical to virtual are profound for all industries, and especially for libraries. The authors have the following three pieces of advice for research libraries: 'they need to make their sites more highly visible in cyberspace by opening them up to search engines; they should abandon any hope of being a one-stop shop; [and] they should accept that much content will seldom or never be used, other than perhaps as a place from which to bounce.'[29]

The University of Auckland Study

As a part of my research on e-books at the University of Auckland, for the LIANZA conference in Auckland in 2004,[30] I gave a questionnaire to library staff and students at the University of Auckland. The goal was to assess the level of knowledge users had about e-books, and what their perceptions of e-books were. For the purpose of this book, I repeated the questionnaire in 2010. My aim this time was to see what had changed over the six years.

Three groups of users were targeted in 2004: library staff, students who enrolled in the library e-book course, and students based at the North Shore campus. The assumption was that students who had enrolled in the e-book course were already aware of and interested in using e-book collections, and that North Shore based students, being distant from the main library, might have more need to use e-books.

Similar groups were targeted in 2010. The questionnaire was administered to library staff and students who had enrolled in the library e-book courses at the end of 2009. Since 2004 the North Shore campus has ceased to exist so in 2010 the questionnaire was given to students in business courses equivalent to the courses that used to be taught at the North Shore campus.

I was tempted to ask some additional questions, and also some different ones, but decided to stick with the 2004 questions so that comparisons could be made.

In 2004, the questions were sent via e-mail in the form of a *Word* document. About half of them were returned as printouts, via internal mail, and half in electronic format via e-mail. This was quite an unintentional finding on user preferences regarding print or electronic communication. Answers received via e-mail were printed out and the printouts saved for further studies. The 2010 answers were gathered via Survey Monkey, but also printed out to be kept with the 2004 answers. Electronic documents from the 2010 study have also been kept.

The targeted groups were not big and the return rate was relatively low. In 2004, library staff returned 16 questionnaires, students who enrolled in e-book courses 33, and students at the North Shore campus 30. In 2010, library staff returned 33 questionnaires, students who enrolled in e-book course 26 (14 undergraduate students, 12 postgraduate), and business students 18 (all undergraduate).

The e-book course and understanding of e-books

The e-book course was organised as one way of promoting e-books, and to help library staff and users gain a better understanding of what e-books are. All three groups were asked if they attended the course. They were also asked if they felt that they had a good understanding of e-books.

More than half of the staff who responded to the 2004 questionnaire had attended the e-book course. About half the students who had enrolled in the e-book course actually attended it. More than half of the students based on North Shore campus had not attended the course.

The majority of respondents in all three groups considered their understanding of e-books to be good. One third of respondents said fair, mostly people who did not attend the course.

In 2010 two-thirds of the Library staff who responded said they had not attended the course. A little over half the students who had expressed interest in the course actually attended it, and only four business students.

As in 2004, most students, whether they attended the course or not, rated their understanding of e-books as good. However, understanding of e-books among library staff was better in 2010 than in 2004. The majority of staff rated their understanding as excellent. Only a few said fair, all people who had not attended the e-book course.

Method of accessing the e-books

The Library provides access to e-books through the library catalogue, course pages (which list recommended readings), directly through e-book databases and via a dedicated e-book

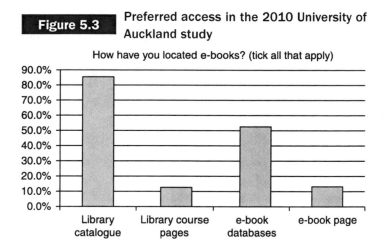

Figure 5.3 Preferred access in the 2010 University of Auckland study

How have you located e-books? (tick all that apply)

page. One of the questions was on the preferred method of access by users.

In 2004, the majority of library staff used the library catalogue to access e-books, while the majority of North Shore based students preferred course pages. The e-book course group was divided. The North Shore based respondents preferred course pages, while the others showed a preference for the library catalogue.

In 2010 (see Figure 5.3), nearly 90 per cent of users across all three groups said that they accessed e-books via the library catalogue. Direct access to e-book databases was chosen by 53 per cent of respondents. Access via course pages was again a popular option among business students.

Print versus electronic

In 2004, all three groups answered that they would prefer print to electronic versions. However, ratios of preference varied. Two-thirds of staff and e-book course students preferred print books, but among the North Shore students, the print version was preferred only by a small margin.

The preference for print format was lower in 2010. Almost two-thirds of staff preferred print books. Almost half the course and business students said that they did not mind if the book was in one or the other format. The other half was almost equally split between the two formats.

The respondents were also asked to explain their preference. Comments did not differ between the two studies. Users prefer print books because they are a familiar format, easier to read, portable and do not require a reading device. Reasons for preferring electronic versions are: 24/7 access, full-text searching, greater availability and online access (particularly appreciated by distance students).

Comments by users who preferred e-books:

'I can cut and paste material for citations and save to my memory stick.' (Library staff)

'I can search faster within the document.' (Student)

'I live too far away to get a physical copy and postage from the university is very slow and expensive to return.' (Student)

'If I lived in Auckland I would probably use the hard copy as I do prefer it.'

'Availablility. Print off bits I need. Access from home.' (Library staff)

Comments by users who preferred print books:

'Difficult to browse on screen and navigate.' (Student)

'It's better for me to read and understand the text, plus making some notes and underlining.' (Student)

'I hate reading online.' (Library staff)

'I hate electronic format.' (Library staff)

'Reading printed material is I think better for one's health.' (Student)

'Both are good, however I may be distracted by using E-book as there are other things on the computer.' (Student)

'I find it too hard on the eyes reading on the computer, and you can't take the computer to bed with you.' (Library staff)

'I do not like reading from a screen for prolonged periods of time. Anything longer than five pages, I would tend towards the print.' (Library staff)

'More reliable.' (Student)

Comments by users who preferred either format:

'I mostly access e-books for Interloan requests. If we are permitted to print from e-books I prefer to use them if possible. For personal/study use I prefer print based because my eyes seem to get tired more when using an e-book and I find it easier to make notes and flick between pages with print books.' (Library staff/Student)

'E-books better for quick access if only needing to look up a part of the text. Print books preferable for intense study.' (Student)

'It depends what I am looking for. If it is just a chapter, it is easier to use the e-book, but if it is information throughout the book, it is more convenient to use the print version.' (Library staff)

'Depending on if I want lots of information from that e-book or not.' (Student)

'If I am working at a computer I would prefer the e-version, but the print version can be carried anywhere.' (Student)

'If the book is available where I am I will look at the print version. If it's at another location or out, I'll look at the e-book version.' (Student)

Both studies confirm that print and e-books are used differently. Many respondents said that e-books were better for quick access if they only needed to look up something in the text, but that print books were preferable for intensive study.

Assuming that many of the students would print out the e-book, one of the questions concerned their awareness of copyright restrictions limiting the number of pages that could be downloaded or copied. In 2004 about one third answered that were not aware of any such restrictions, while in 2010 eighty per cent of users were aware of copyright restrictions, with undergraduate students being the least aware.

Importance of e-book features

Different e-book features were rated differently (Figure 5.4). In 2004, access anytime, anywhere was regarded as very important by a majority of course students, and by almost all

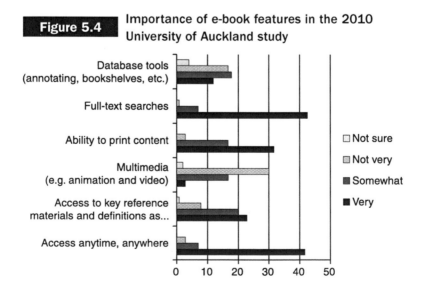

Figure 5.4 Importance of e-book features in the 2010 University of Auckland study

staff. Access to key reference materials and definitions as one reads the e-book was valued more by library staff than by both groups of students. All three groups assumed that elements such as animation or video are of little importance. However, students found these features more useful than library staff. Ability to print content was regarded as very important by a majority of students and staff. Almost all library staff rated access to searchable content as very important. Some students agreed, but not all.

In 2010, all groups considered as important 24/7 access, full-text searches and ability to print content. Access to key reference materials and definitions as one reads the e-book was also highly valued by all. All three groups assumed that elements such as animation or video and database tools (annotating, bookshelves, etc.) are of little importance.

Frequency of use

The library staff used e-books more often than the other two groups in the 2004 study. Both the North Shore based students and course students said that they used e-books once a month or less often. Only a few of the respondents said that they used e-books more than once a week. In 2010, all groups said that they mostly access e-books once a month, or less than once a month (see Figure 5.5).

The users were also asked if they would like more e-books in their subject areas. In 2004 the majority of all three groups answered yes. In 2010 almost all the students answered yes, along with 76 per cent of library staff.

Some of the 'other comments'

The questionnaires provided an opportunity to add 'other comments'. In both studies users complained about a lack of

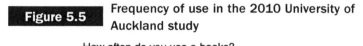

Figure 5.5 Frequency of use in the 2010 University of Auckland study

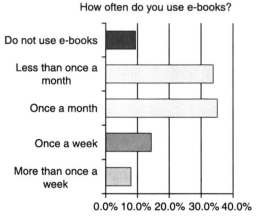

How often do you use e-books?

- Do not use e-books
- Less than once a month
- Once a month
- Once a week
- More than once a week

0.0% 10.0% 20.0% 30.0% 40.0%

standards and relevant titles. Several subject librarians mentioned that they liked the fact that they are able to search across whole collections, not just within a single book, and that e-books are incredibly useful for titles that are in high demand.

Because of the small sample sizes findings in these two studies are not generalisable. However, the data does suggest some trends.

Library staff who responded were more familiar with e-books in 2010 than in 2004, but interestingly, students do not seem to have a better understanding of e-books than in 2004. This seems strange considering that students should have had more exposure to the medium in 2010 than six years ago. While library staff still prefer print books, students are opting for convenience – most of them do not mind what format the book is in as long as it is relevant and available.

Changes are noticeable in access paths as well. In 2010, all three groups preferred the library catalogue. This, again, could be convenience – users do not have to perform separate searches to locate the books in the first place. The questionnaires did not ask about reasons for using e-books, so we do not know if it was for research, or leisure, or something else. Nor do we know how long they spent reading. There is much scope for further research.

Usage statistics

Thorough information about the use of library collections is important so libraries can meet user needs and make changes to collection policies. Library budgets are tight, even more so in the last few years, and information about the use of collections for which libraries pay ongoing subscriptions is essential for making decisions about which collections should be retained and which subscriptions should be cancelled. Librarians are mostly concerned about the usage of e-books with annual subscriptions, and think that they do not need to monitor collections with perpetual access. But usage statistics are also helpful in making decisions on which collections are worth spending money on for cataloguing, or promotion and training.

According to *ebrary's Global eBook Survey*[31] the primary decisions influenced by usage statistics were decisions related to acquisition: renewal (59 per cent), budget allocation (59 per cent) and title acquisition (53 per cent). Only 33 per cent of libraries mentioned training, which indicates that only one third of the librarians who responded to the survey acknowledge a connection between usage and training. However, in the survey analysis, Allen McKiel suggests that 'in cases where usage is low, instruction rather than cancellation might be the remedy'.[32]

Collecting statistics can be a labour-intensive task, and successfully tracking, comparing and analysing usage statistics can be quite challenging. For libraries with multiple collections it is an even bigger task. A number of libraries gather usage data locally from library systems and OPACs (online public access catalogues). However, this data is limited to the number of times traffic went to the publisher database. Libraries cannot track what is happening in the database itself, and they have to rely on the statistical data provided by vendors and publishers.

Not all e-book providers make online usage statistics available. Statistics are offered only for commercial collections, and not even for all of them. In the 2009 Association of Learned and Professional Society Publishers (ALPSP) survey on scholarly book publishing practices, only 52.9 per cent of publishers reported that they supply usage statistics to their customers. Large publishers are the most likely to provide usage statistics, with 93.3 per cent doing so.[33]

Publishers' statistical data is obtainable in a variety of ways. In most cases statistics are provided on the publisher's website. Someone in the library has to keep track of the various URLs and passwords necessary for retrieving usage statistics. Where statistics are not available online they have to regularly chase providers for updated statistics.

Data provided by publishers and vendors is not presented in a standard way. Some of the most common parameters in reports are:

- the number of sessions, where a user session is the period from entering to leaving a database;
- the duration of sessions;
- the number of times a particular title was accessed;
- the number of full-text content units accessed;
- the number of pages viewed.

Lack of consistency in the data they deliver makes comparison between different databases difficult.

Once collected and collated, often through tedious manual manipulations of spreadsheets, the analysis of the data presents further challenges. The terminology used by vendors varies, and the definitions of searches and sessions are open to interpretation. Nor can numbers alone inform librarians whether users retrieved the information they were looking for and whether it was sufficient or too much. Many authors studying e-book usage have highlighted the need for consistency in usage statistics between vendors, among them Millie Jackson,[34] Ellen Safley[35] and John Cox.[36]

There are two initiatives in the area of standards for e-book usage statistics: COUNTER (Counting Online Usage of NeTworked Electronic Resources)[37] and SUSHI (Standardised Usage Statistics Harvesting Initiative).[38]

COUNTER is a set of open, international standards and protocols for recording and exchanging vendor-generated usage statistics. It has standards for journal databases, e-books and reference works. Talking about the future of COUNTER, Peter Shepherd, COUNTER Project Director, said:

> It has become clear that neither librarians nor vendors want COUNTER to develop an ever more complex set of standards and procedures for measuring online usage statistics. Therefore COUNTER's main goal for the future will be to develop and maintain a set of relatively simple usage reports that can be implemented by most vendors, for all the major online content categories purchased by libraries: journals, databases, reference works and books.[39]

The COUNTER organisation was formed in 2002 and, according to Marthyn Borghuis, Senior Manager, Elsevier Usage Research Department, by the middle of 2004, COUNTER-compliant vendors accounted for more than 50 per cent of the annual output of STM [Science, Technology, Medicine] full-text articles and database abstracts.[40]

However, not all publishers and vendors have recognised the value of the COUNTER e-book code of practice. According to a 2009 ALPSP survey, 52.9 per cent of publishers reported that they provide usage statistics to their customers, but only 40 per cent provide such data in COUNTER-compliant form, most of them being large publishers. Commercial publishers are more likely to provide usage statistics and these statistics are far more likely to be COUNTER-compliant than those from non-profit publishers.[41]

SUSHI is a NISO (National Information Standards Organisation) initiative which aims to automate the delivery of COUNTER-formatted statistics. It is a retrieval protocol which should save the need for visiting lots of websites and manually downloading usage data on a vendor-by-vendor basis. It is a SOAP (Simple Object Access Portal) request/response web services 'wrapper' for the XML version of COUNTER reports. It works best with an ERM (Electronic Resource Management) system acting as the client, thus facilitating the downloading of usage data into a system already populated with bibliographic, financial and licencing data.

By enabling the standardisation and automation of e-book data collection, these two initiatives promise to significantly reduce the labour involved in retrieving and analysing usage data. Jenny Walker, executive vice-president for Xrefer, advocating compliance, says that 'as publishers and aggregators develop new ebook and reference work platforms, they should ensure that COUNTER compliance is a non-negotiable requirement from the outset. Many providers now releasing ebooks already offer COUNTER-compliant ejournal and database usage statistics, and this experience should be applied to the ebook platforms. COUNTER standardisation is what librarians need and want, and librarians should be actively demanding compliance of all their vendors'.[42]

An Association of Research Libraries (ARL) survey found that 83 per cent of member libraries monitor the usage of e-books while 17 per cent do not. Most libraries rely on statistics provided by e-book vendors and publishers; however, these statistics vary in quality. Collected data varies and includes numbers of downloads, pages viewed, copied, and printed; numbers of successful searches; and numbers of searches turned away.[43]

Statistics can be collected from vendor sites by an external provider working on the library's behalf. This saves a lot of time as libraries do not have to go to vendor sites themselves. The University of Auckland Library uses ScholarlyStats to obtain statistical data from databases from the 24 selected vendors. However, as different vendors count usage differently, not all 24 vendors are represented in each report. Although these reports contain accurate counts, one has to be aware that some journals and books are provided by multiple vendors and figures from different vendors are not consolidated.

Statistics of e-books usage offer only limited help in understanding e-book user behaviour, and are often difficult to compare, but they are a good indicator of use and a good way of obtaining information about usage trends.

Figures 5.6 and 5.7 show statistics of the usage of *netLibrary* and *ebrary* at the University of Auckland Library from the purchase of the collections until the end of 2009. On various occasions when I was speaking about the University of Auckland Library e-book collections, I looked

Figure 5.6 *netLibrary* usage at the University of Auckland Library, 2001–2009

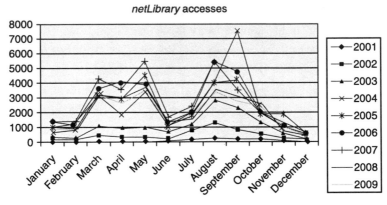

Figure 5.7 *ebrary* usage at the University of Auckland Library, 2002–2009

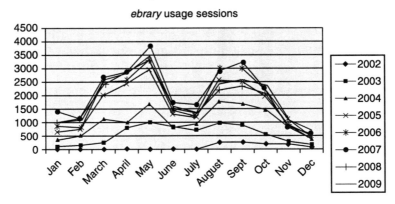

at the usage of *netLibrary* and *ebrary*. I chose these two because they were the earliest collections purchased, and because their content is interdisciplinary.

Statistical data shows that usage of these collections correlates with the academic year and that they are more heavily used when assignments are due. A handful of titles were prescribed as recommended reading for large undergraduate courses and were accessed hundreds of times. For example, the book *Ethics and Corporate Social Responsibility: Why Giants Fall*, by Ronald R. Sims was accessed over 500 times in April and May 2006. This reflects the findings of the user surveys mentioned earlier in the chapter which show that e-books are mainly used for research and study.

Table 5.1 and Figure 5.8 represent month-by-month usage of the *ebrary* collection in 2009. In the questionnaire many respondents to the University of Auckland study expressed their preference for print over e-format. Monthly statistics for 2009 show that between 3.41 per cent and 9.31 per cent of viewed pages were printed (on average, 6.16 per cent over the whole year). Between 0.56 per cent and 2.74 per cent of pages viewed were also copied electronically (on average, 1.64 per cent). Figures also show that between one and three

Table 5.1	*ebrary* usage at the University of Auckland Library in 2009

2009	Unique sessions	Unique documents	Pages viewed	Pages viewed per document	Pages copied	Pages printed
Jan	1,789	1,008	34,206	33.93	937	2,458
Feb	546	1,066	31,287	29.34	573	1,861
Mar	2,005	2,591	86,690	33.45	1,249	6,256
Apr	1,810	2,823	88,459	31.33	1,722	4,968
May	2,458	3,517	117,418	33.38	2,714	4,003
Jun	739	1,607	46,430	28.89	865	1,952
Jul	668	1,334	37,397	28.03	636	3,005
Aug	1,718	2,447	80,887	33.05	863	3,809
Sep	1,390	2,559	80,044	31.27	956	3,340
Oct	1,228	2378	75,647	31.81	1,157	4,396
Nov	407	1044	30,478	29.19	170	2,838
Dec	190	651	14,540	22.33	230	1,212

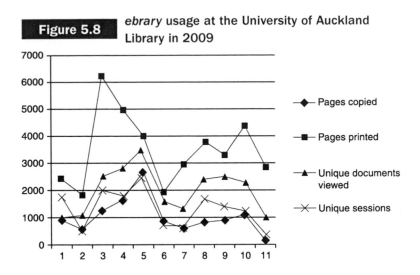

Figure 5.8 *ebrary* usage at the University of Auckland Library in 2009

documents were seen per session, and that between 22 and 33 pages were viewed per document.

Table 5.2 provides *Safari* statistics. The library has only around 200 titles in *Safari*, but the collection remains relevant as *Safari* allows us to replace less-used titles with more popular ones. These statistics show that users spend only four to eight minutes per session (the time between entering a database and leaving it). This correlates closely with user surveys that show that e-books are not read cover to cover, but rather used to quickly locate necessary information.

SpringerLink usage statistics at the University of Auckland Library are shown in Figure 5.9. They highlight the importance of having metadata available in the library catalogue. The big jump in usage at the end of 2007 is a result of loading bibliographic records provided by Springer into the library catalogue. However, these records did not comply with MARC standards and AACR2 and in April 2009, Springer's records were replaced by records created by OCLC. This is reflected in the increased usage in 2009. Peaks in April 2008 and 2009 are due to several titles being used as recommended reading.

Table 5.2 *Safari* statistics of usage at the University of Auckland Library

	2004	2005	2006	2007	2008	2009
Sessions	934	1,690	1,531	2,497	2,105	2,224
Sections	6,581	12,046	9,922	13,660	12,790	20,262
Time	6:37	8:35	6:50	4:09	4:19	7:23
Searches	519	569	631	720	687	13,01
Rejected sessions	0	0	0	8	29	195

Figure 5.9 *SpringerLink* usage at the University of Auckland Library, 2007–2009

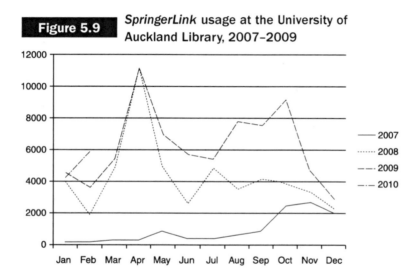

The University of Auckland Library statistics provide comparisons only at a very basic level. More detailed usage data and user observation would be very helpful. A number of studies have examined e-book usage in academic libraries more closely. Particularly interesting is research that compares usage statistics for electronic and print books in an effort to better understand user preferences for one format over the other.

Justin Littman and Lynn Silipigni Connaway compared usage of 7,880 print books and their electronic counterparts at Duke University Libraries. The survey was published in 2004. They found that e-books received 11 per cent more use than print books – of 7,880 titles available in both print and electronic versions 3,158 e-book titles and 2,799 print titles were used during the study period. They reported that 1,688 titles were used in both print and e-book format, 1,484 titles were used in e-book format, but not in print, and 1,125 titles were used in print, but not e-book format; 3,597 titles were used in neither format. Print book usage was measured by check-outs and e-book usage by 'accesses'. The authors concluded that there are several things librarians should bear in mind when planning for e-book collection development. They suggested that attention should be paid to titles that benefit from the extra functionality offered by an electronic format, such as reference books, and note that e-books may provide more benefits in certain subject areas. They also said that e-books are excellent candidates for additional copy purchases when print copies of titles are receiving heavy usage.[44]

A similar study was done at Louisiana State University by Marilyn Christianson and Marsha Aucoin. They examined usage statistics over a one-year period for 2,852 print and e-book equivalents. The study was carried out in 2002. The study demonstrated that print book use did not necessarily predict e-book use, or vice versa. The usage of print and electronic books is shown in Figure 5.10, and confirms that use of e-books is closely related to assignment writing. Print books were used more than e-books, and e-book use was more concentrated in fewer titles. The authors also noted differences in user preferences by subject area with library science, literature, economics and business being among the most popular e-book subjects. However, the relationship

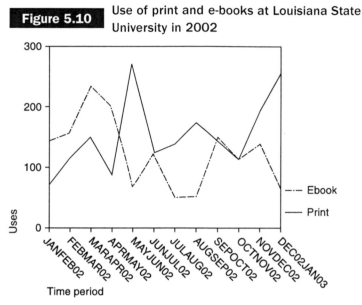

Figure 5.10 Use of print and e-books at Louisiana State University in 2002

Source: Christianson, M., & Aucoin, M. (2005) 'Electronic or print books: which are used?' *Library Collections, Acquisitions, & Technical Services,* 29(1).

between use of print and electronic books was not linear, and the authors concluded that more studies need to be done in order to better understand what is happening.[45]

Two studies analysed the usage of print and e-books at Auburn University in Montgomery. Timothy P. Bailey measured *netLibrary* usage from 2000 to 2004, and reported that e-book usage steadily grew over the five-year period, while use of the print collection decreased. Some of the increase in e-book use was attributed to the addition of new *netLibrary* collections during the study period.[46] Karen Williams and Rickey Best compared the usage of 323 titles available in both print and e-format over a one-year period. This study analysed circulation patterns for electronic books in the fields of Political Science, Public Administration and Law, and found that print was still the preferred format and that e-book usage fits a power curve, with small areas of exceptionally high use and larger areas of low to no use. Most e-books received no use during the study period.[47]

Nancy Sprague and Ben Hunter used statistical data to ascertain the cost of individual e-books. They conducted an in-depth analysis of three major electronic book providers at the University of Idaho Library in 2008. Usage statistics showed relatively low use of e-books across both subject areas and platforms. They found that

> our cost [was] $1.97 per title. This extremely low cost is offset somewhat by our low usage statistics, which bring our cost per use to $3.67/use. Our individually purchased titles had much higher usage than our package titles, but the high average individual price translated into a per-use cost over 17 times that of our package e-books. However, it should be noted that individually purchased titles are one-time cost and perpetual use, so over time the gap between per-use price of packages and individual titles will probably narrow. Our cost and subject analyses yielded valuable information, but our usage statistics revealed some of the most interesting and unexpected results. We found that less than 20 per cent of our e-books have ever been accessed (16 per cent of *Ebrary* titles and 27 per cent of *NetLibrary* titles), and less than 2 per cent of our books have had repeated usage (more than five accesses).[48]

Book publishers also monitor statistics. Springer's 2007 study of usage metrics confirms a positive trend in user adoption of e-books. The *SpringerLink* website includes both e-books and e-journals and the study compared their usage. This is interesting as e-books are often contrasted with e-journals. The study found that e-books accounted for roughly a quarter of the total usage on the *SpringerLink* website in the first year of Springer's e-books programme. The study also confirmed that institutions which were early adopters of e-books had higher e-book usage figures. In some institution e-books were used as often as e-journals.[49]

A number of other studies have been done. The studies mentioned here are the ones I have personally found the most interesting. Together with usage data from the University of Auckland Library, I hope that they have successfully demonstrated the insights usage statistics can deliver, and proved the importance of giving them due attention.

Notes and references

1. Johnson, L., Levine, A., Smith, R. and Stone, S. (2010) *2010 Horizon Report.* Retrieved 4 July 2010 from *http://www.educause.edu/ELI/2010HorizonReport/ 195400.*
2. Nelson, M.R. (2008) 'E-books in higher education: nearing the end of the era of hype?' *EDUCAUSE Review*, 43(2). Retrieved 4 July 2010 from *http://www. educause.edu/EDUCAUSE+Review/EDUCAUSE ReviewMagazineVolume43/EBooksinHigherEducation Nearing/162677.*
3. Ibid.
4. *eBooks – The End User Perspective* (2008) Retrieved 4 July 2010 from *http://www.springer.com/cda/content/ document/cda_downloaddocument/eBooks+-+the+End +User+Experience?SGWID=0-0-45-608298-0.*
5. Dinkelman, A. and Stacy-Bates, K. (2007) 'Accessing e-Books through academic library web sites', *College and Research Libraries*, 68(1), 45–57.

6. See *http://www.library.auckland.ac.nz/ebooks/*.

7. See *http://www.library.auckland.ac.nz/instruct/ebook/ ebook.htm*.

8. See *http://www.library.auckland.ac.nz/docs/handouts/ e-book.pdf*.

9. See *http://www.cityu.edu.hk/lib/ebook_conf/erall_ intro.htm*.

10. See *http://www.abdn.ac.uk/library/vodcasts.shtml*.

11. McGeachin, R.B. and Ramirez, D. (2006) 'Collaborating with students to develop an advertising campaign', *College & Undergraduate Libraries*, 12(1–2).

12. Anson, C. and Connell, R.R. (2009) *E-book Collections*. Washington, DC: Association of Research Libraries.

13. Levine-Clark, M. (2006) 'Electronic book usage: a survey at the University of Denver', *Libraries and the Academy*, 6(3).

14. Rowlands, I., Nicholas, D., Jamali, H.R. and Hutlington, P. (2007) 'What do faculty and students really think about e-books?', *ASLIB Proceedings*, 59(6), 489–511. Retrieved 4 July 2010 from *http://www.homepages.ucl. ac.uk/~uczciro/findings.pdf*.

15. *eBooks – The End User Perspective* (2008) Retrieved 4 July 2010 from *http://www.springer.com/cda/content/ document/cda_downloaddocument/eBooks+-+the+End +User+Experience?SGWID=0-0-45-608298-0*.

16. Renner, R.A. (2007) *eBooks – Costs and Benefits to Academic and Research Libraries*. Retrieved 4 July 2010 from *http://www.springer.com/cda/content/document/ cda_downloaddocument/eBook+White+Paper. pdf?SGWID=0-0-45-415198-0*.

17. *2008 Global Student E-book Survey Sponsored by ebrary*. (2008) Retrieved 4 July 2010 from *http://www. ebrary.com/corp/collateral/en/Survey/ebrary_student_ survey_2008.pdf*.

18. More about JISC national e-books observatory project and all reports can be found at *http://www.jiscebooksproject.org/reports*.

19. JISC (2008) *Findings from the First User Survey.* Retrieved 4 July 2010 from *http://www.jiscebooksproject.org/wp-content/e-books-project-first-user-survey-a4-final-version.pdf*.

20. JISC (2009) *Headline Findings from the User Surveys: CIBER Final Report.* Retrieved 4 July 2010 from *http://www.jiscebooksproject.org/reports*.

21. JISC (2009) *JISC National E-book Observatory Project: Key Findings and Recommendations: Final Report, November 2009.* Retrieved 4 July 2010 from *http://www.jiscebooksproject.org/reports/finalreport*.

22. JISC defines deep log analysis as 'a methodology that helps librarians, publishers and other suppliers of web-based content to a better understanding of how consumers actually use their services. By analysing raw transactional server-side logs, CIBER is able to develop a series of user metrics that describe how users interact with the system: for example, session length, number of content or other pages viewed, whether or not an internal search engine was used, which titles and subjects were viewed and when an access took place. This data reflects what people actually do online and not what they think they did or what they think they ought to say to a researcher.' From *http://www.jiscebooksproject.org/deep-log-analysis/what-is-deep-log-analysis* (accessed 4 July 2010).

23. All documents and reports related to JISC studies are available at *http://www.jiscebooksproject.org/*.

24. JISC disciplines are Media Studies, Medicine, Engineering, and Business and Management.

25. Hernon, P., Hopper, R., Leach, M.R., Saunders, L.L. and Zhang, J. (2007) 'E-book use by students: undergraduates

in economics, literature, and nursing', *Journal of Academic Librarianship*, 33(1).

26. Buzzetto-More, N., Sweat-Guy, R. and Elobaid, M. (2007) 'Reading in a digital age: e-books are students ready for this learning object?' *Interdisciplinary Journal of Knowledge and Learning Objects*, 3. Retrieved 4 July 2010 from *http://ijello.org/Volume3/IJKLOv3p239-250Buzzetto.pdf*.

27. Gregory, C.L. (2008) ' "But I want a real book": an investigation of undergraduates' usage and attitudes toward electronic books', *Reference and User Services Quarterly*, 47(3).

28. Carlock, D.M. and Perry, A.M. (2008) 'Exploring faculty experiences with e-books: a focus group', *Library Hi Tech*, 26(2). Retrieved 4 July 2010 from *http://www. emeraldinsight.com/Insight/viewContentItem.do;jsessio nid=AE0043C2507D5C69EE77C4CD22CD4B45? contentType=Article&hdAction=lnkpdf&conten tId=1729333*.

29. *Information Behaviour of the Researcher of the Future: A CIBER Briefing Paper* (2008). Retrieved 4 July 2010 from *http://www.jisc.ac.uk/media/documents/programmes/ reppres/gg_final_keynote_11012008.pdf*.

30. Obradovic, K. (2004) *E-books – Essentials or Extras? The University of Auckland Library Experience.* Paper presented at the LIANZA Conference. Retrieved 6 July 2010 from *http://researchspace.auckland.ac.nz/handle/ 2292/3391*.

31. *ebrary's Global eBook Survey* (2007). Retrieved 4 July 2010 from *http://www.ebrary.com/corp/collateral/en/ Survey/ebrary_eBook_survey_2007.pdf*.

32. Ibid.

33. Cox, J. and Cox, L. (2010) *Scholarly Book Publishing Practice: An ALPSP Survey of Academic Book*

Publishers' Policies and Practices, First Survey, 2009. Shoreham-by-Sea: Association of Learned and Professional Society Publishers.

34. Jackson, M. (2007) 'One by one or bundle by bundle', *Against the Grain*, 19(2).

35. Safley, E. (2006) 'Demand for e-books in an academic library', *Journal of Library Administration*, 45(3/4).

36. Cox, J. (2008) 'Making sense of e-book usage data', *The Acquisitions Librarian*, 19(3/4).

37. See *http://www.projectcounter.org/*.

38. See *http://www.niso.org/workrooms/sushi*.

39. Borghuis, M. (2005) 'How COUNTER continues to help librarians and vendors make sense of usage reports', *Library Connect*, 7(8-9). Retrieved 4 July 2010 from *http://libraryconnect.elsevier.com/lcp/0701/lcp070112.html*.

40. Ibid.

41. Cox, J. and Cox, L. (2010) *Scholarly Book Publishing Practice: An ALPSP survey of Academic Book Publishers' Policies and Practices, First Survey, 2009.* Shoreham-by-Sea: Association of Learned and Professional Society Publishers.

42. Walker, J. (2007) 'COUNTER: getting the measure of e-books', *eLucidate*, 4(3). Retrieved 6 July 2010 from *http://corp.credoreference.com/images/PDFs/article_counter_ukeig.pdf*.

43. Anson, C. and Connell, R.R. (2009) *E-book Collections.* Washington, DC: Association of Research Libraries.

44. Littman, J. and Connaway, L.S. (2004) 'A circulation analysis of print books and e-books in an academic research library', *Library Resources and Technical Services*, 48(4).

45. Christianson, M. and Aucoin, M. (2005) 'Electronic or print books: which are used?' *Library Collections, Acquisitions, & Technical Services*, 29(1).

46. Bailey, P. (2006) 'Electronic book usage at a master's level I university: a longitudinal study', *Journal of Academic Librarianship*, 32(1).

47. Williams, K.C. and Best, R. (2006) 'E-book usage and the choice outstanding academic book list: is there a correlation?' *Journal of Academic Librarianship*, 32(5).

48. Sprague, N. and Hunter, B. (2008) 'Assessing e-books: taking a closer look at e-book statistics Library Collections', *Acquisitions, and Technical Services*, 32(3–4).

49. *eBooks – The End User Perspective* (2008). Retrieved 4 July 2010 from *http://www.springer.com/cda/content/ document/cda_downloaddocument/eBooks+-+the+End +User+Experience?SGWID=0-0-45-608298-0.*

6

New opportunities

E-books have been recognised as having great potential to be an effective and efficient educational tool. The combination of text with animations, graphics, simulations and sounds can be very useful in explaining abstract theories and concepts. E-book features such as hyperlinks, customisability of text size and the ability to convert text to audio also have benefits in education.

The previous chapter has shown that the use of e-books in academic institutions is closely related to the academic year and that they are used to locate specific information rather than for linear reading. That indicates that e-books are well suited for research purposes. This chapter will look further into e-books as learning objects and their potential in modern education.

New ways of teaching and learning

The face of learning is rapidly changing as digital technology is employed in an ever-increasing range of roles. Information technology now supports virtually every aspect of higher education, including finances, security and sustainability, as well as teaching and research. Computers and computer-assisted instruction are becoming indispensable. The great majority of universities now have a course management system (CMS) or a virtual learning environment (VLE) of some kind, designed to support teaching and learning.

The extensive use of computers and the Internet in educational institutions is reflected in the growth of online learning. The development of smartphones has enabled mobile learning, i.e. learning with mobile devices. Nowadays there are hardly any traditional classrooms without at least some kind of electronic tools to support learning.

A survey done at three universities in Glasgow in 2003 on the use of computer-based learning materials among teaching staff found that 67 per cent of lecturers delivered course material electronically, and 63 per cent included electronic material on reading lists. The study also found that undergraduate teachers were more likely than postgraduate or evening class tutors to deliver electronic course material and to recommend electronic material to students.[1]

The Sloan Consortium[2] has run an annual survey on online education in the United States since 2003. The survey attempts to answer questions about the nature and extent of online education. Allen and Seaman, who compiled the 2009 report, define online courses as those in which at least 80 per cent of the course content is delivered online. The survey confirmed that online course enrolments have continued to grow at rates far in excess of the total higher education student population, and this growth shows no signs of slowing. According to the survey, over 4.6 million higher education students (over 25 per cent of the total) were taking at least one online course during the fall 2008 term, which was a 17 per cent increase over 2007. Attitudes to online learning have become more positive since they were first measured in 2003 (Figure 6.1), with the percentage of chief academic officers in the United States who rated learning outcomes for online courses compared to face-to-face as 'Same', 'Somewhat Superior', or 'Superior' having increased from 57 per cent to 68 per cent.[3]

Figure 6.1 Learning outcomes in online education compared to face-to-face education, according to the Sloan Consortium 2009 survey

	2003	2004	2006	2009
Superior	0.6%	1.0%	1.8%	2.1%
Somewhat superior	11.7%	10.0%	15.1%	12.4%
Same	44.9%	50.6%	45.0%	53.0%
Somewhat inferior	32.1%	28.4%	30.3%	23.0%
Inferior	10.7%	10.1%	7.8%	9.5%

The most frequently mentioned advantages of computer-based courses over traditional lectures and tutorials are:

- *Convenience and flexibility.* Learners do not have to physically attend classes. With learning sessions available 24×7 they can work through modules at their own pace.

- *Personalised learning experience.* Learning can be tailored to suit individual learning needs.

- *Time-saving.* Instructions delivered electronically reduce the amount of time that learners spend on tasks.

The *Global Digital Economy – E-Government, E-Health and E-Education Trends for 2009* report, produced by Paul Budde Communication, predicts further growth in e-learning, giving as the reason the fact that more educational institutions will be encouraged to explore e-learning as a cheaper alternative to classroom-style training.[4]

In line with the ideal of free access to knowledge, many universities allow free access to their classroom materials. Sharing classroom materials allows students to engage with eminent experts in their fields, and experts to have the opportunity of promoting their ideas to the whole world. For example, the MIT OpenCourseWare site makes virtually all MIT course content available on the web, free of charge.[5]

Applications of e-learning technologies in formal education are continually evolving. A multitude of e-learning tools are now available. Some are specifically designed to create a shell in which to organise instructional content. Virtual learning environments (VLE), described as online classrooms, allow students to access relevant information easily and quickly. Just about any computer application can be an e-learning delivery or collaboration tool. Web 2.0 tools, also called social software, are used with increasing frequency, and blogs and wikis are becoming quite common. The most popular tools are electronic library databases and websites. As part of the new and exciting electronic world, e-books also encourage students to be more engaged in learning tasks.

E-books have been highly valued for their promises of enhancing e-learning and distance education. Shiratuddin et al. explored e-book technology in relation to its applications in distance education. They used a remote testing approach and asked a group of students who had no prior e-book reading experience to submit assignments (typical students' tasks) in Microsoft Reader format. The study proved that e-books can enhance the interaction between educators and students in the exchange of teaching and learning materials.[6]

The modern world is computer-oriented and loaded with information. This puts pressure on educators and highlights the responsibility they have to effectively integrate technologies and information literacy into their curricula. Jeremy Shapiro and Shelley Hughes said in 1996 that information literacy should be conceived more broadly as a new liberal art that extends from knowing how to use computers and access information to critical reflection on the nature of information itself, its technical infrastructure and its social, cultural, and philosophical context and impact.[7]

Other authors point out that it is important to make a distinction between information literacy and information technology. One of the messages of the collection of essays, *Information and IT literacy*, is that information literacy rather than IT literacy is the key to enabling learning in the twenty-first century.[8]

Information is available through many channels and often comes unfiltered. The authenticity, validity and reliability of that information are often uncertain. Students have to acquire the skills, strategies and insights to successfully exploit the rapidly changing information and communication technologies that continually emerge in the world. It is important to teach students information literacy from their freshman years so that they can start their university careers with the tools they need to succeed. When students are able to understand and evaluate information they can use it in their studies, and also in their workplaces and lives. In the twenty-first century a person must be able to recognise when information is needed and have the ability to locate, evaluate and use it effectively.

A 2008 CIBER briefing paper on the information behaviour of the researcher of the future shows that young people are having great difficulties in navigating and profiting from the virtual scholarly environment. The paper highlights the need to teach information skills.[9] And, in fact, literacy educators of all grade levels are recognising the need to respond to the changing array of media technologies and resources, both within and outside the classroom, to make education more responsive to today's learning needs.

In 2009 the Primary Research Group did a survey on use of library reference, information literacy and subject specialists by higher education faculty. Over 70 per cent of the respondents said that they had incorporated some form of information literacy instruction into their teaching, designed to help students to better familiarise themselves with library resources in their field. The study found that United States faculty (72 per cent) were significantly more likely to have done so than faculty in Canada (53.5 per cent). Also, faculty at research universities (57.3 per cent) were the least likely among the various types of colleges to have added an information literacy component. The larger the college, the less likely faculty were to include an information literacy dimension in their teaching: 76.67 per cent of faculty at colleges with fewer than 1,000 students but only 61.8 per cent of faculty at colleges with more than 20,000 students embedded the use of information and communications technologies within their curricula. Faculty in psychology and counselling, as well as in education, were more likely than others to include information literacy in teaching. The study also noted that the tendency to include an information literacy component in teaching was strongly related to the overall tendency of the faculty member to use the library.[10]

A strategic priority for academic libraries is to create an environment that supports teaching, research and learning. With the changing nature of tertiary education and the growing interest in the creation of new types of learning environments, new roles for libraries are also emerging. Libraries are developing new services for new types of students. Establishing student learning commons, digitising course materials and providing course management systems are just some of the initiatives.

Another important role for modern academic libraries is acquiring access to high-demand electronic material. Although many digital resources are created and maintained locally by scholars and research groups, a larger number, particularly materials of more general interest, are captured in the more formal systems of publishers, digital libraries and institutional repositories. In this context, e-books and other electronic resources create an opportunity for libraries to align closely with the teaching and learning priorities of their universities.

Since 2000, Ithaka's Faculty Surveys have examined how new technologies are impacting on faculty attitudes and behaviours. The 2009 survey shows that faculty see their libraries as very important in buying (90 per cent) and archiving (70 per cent). They also perceive themselves as becoming decreasingly dependent on the library for their research and teaching needs.[11]

According to the 2006 Ithaka survey, a minority of faculty members used e-books (16 per cent occasionally, 36 per cent rarely). Enthusiasm for e-books was noticeably higher among librarians than faculty, 13 per cent of faculty and half of the librarians viewing them as very important for research or teaching at the time. A further 24 per cent of faculty and more than two-thirds of the librarians expected them to be very important in five years' time. Both librarians and faculty members saw the two formats as complementary, rather than e-books substituting for print books. Commenting on the results of the 2006 survey, Schonfeld and Guthrie said that

> based on other findings, it often seems that the expectations of the research universities may be predictive of broader patterns, but for now, it is reasonable to conclude that library acquisitions practices are generally not responding to faculty members' demand for e-books but rather to students' demand or perhaps to expected future demand from faculty.[12]

The 2009 Ithaka survey showed that e-books continued to be regarded as marginal by scholars as tools for their research and

Figure 6.2 Faculty ratings of the importance of various materials for research and teaching in the 2009 Ithaka survey

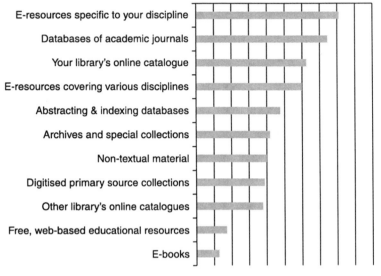

teaching (Figure 6.2). Only 13 per cent of the faculty members rated them as important for their research and study. However, the percentage of faculty members who expected e-books to be important in five years' time has increased, compared to the 2006 survey, from 24 to 31 per cent, and about half of respondents said that long-term e-book preservation is very important (see Figure 6.3). Schonfeld and Housewright, who compiled the report, think that this suggests that it may still be early days for scholarly monographs in digital format.[13]

A new kind of 'book'

The electronic environment raises the possibility of integrating a wide range of different kinds of content including text,

Figure 6.3 Faculty ratings of the importance of various materials for preservation and for research and teaching in the 2009 Ithaka survey

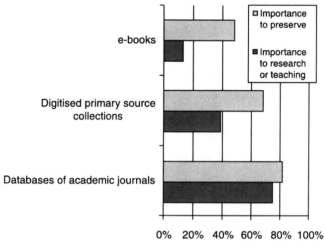

images, videos, animations, audio, simulations and remote and virtual experiments. An electronic book that has text enriched by multimedia is non-linear and is far more than a book in the traditional sense.

As noted earlier, there is disagreement between authors in their understanding of the nature of the e-book, and to what extent it should mirror classical book structure to qualify as a 'book'. What, indeed, does the familiar concept of a book really imply? The *Oxford English Dictionary* defines a book as 'a written or printed work consisting of pages glued or sewn together along one side and bound in covers'.[14] Wikipedia says that 'a book is a set or collection of written, printed, illustrated, or blank sheets, made of paper, parchment, or other various material, usually fastened together to hinge at one side'.[15]

Both definitions imply that the content within the structure in which it is bound forms a complete text in itself. Transferred to the electronic environment, both these definitions allow the e-book to be more than just a mirror of a print book. If we replace the idea of 'pages glued together' with an 'electronic container', we are left with the content, i.e. a work consisting of written text and (digital) illustrations.

Electronic books can closely imitate print books, but they can also be very different, because of additional functionalities that print by its nature cannot have. Text and digital features can be integrated to various degrees, sometimes to the extent that there is almost no difference between an e-book and a website.

Texts enriched by multimedia can be a very powerful support in teaching and learning. Some examples of educational tools where multimedia is used in combination with educational texts are listed below. These 'books' have been developed to support university courses and they allow students to explore and experience the content in rich, interactive formats.

Visualising Electricity & Magnetism

In conjunction with Ball State University, the Massachusetts Institute of Technology (MIT) has produced an electronic textbook called *Visualizing Electricity & Magnetism*.[16] The book was designed as part of the Technology-Enabled Active Learning (TEAL) project.[17] The authors, John Belcher and Jennifer George-Palilonis, use as little mathematics as possible, and instead explain electricity and magnetism in pictures, movies and interactive computer visualisation. Their aim was to develop a tool that will help students to visualise concepts that are normally invisible to the naked eye.

The book is designed for an introductory electricity and magnetism course, and explains field theory, scalar and vector fields, electrostatics, magnetostatics, Faraday's Law and light. It combines visual storytelling, animation, graphic design and nonlinear presentation and includes 3D animations, interactive applets and videos.

The intention of the TEAL Project is to transform the way physics is taught in large enrolment physics classes and to decrease failure rates. The results show that learning outcomes are significantly better than those obtained in traditional teaching environments. Visualisation helps students improve their conceptual understanding of the subject matter, which results in lower failure rates.[18]

Français interactif

The Texas Language Technology Center[19] at the University of Texas, Austin, has implemented new technologies in foreign language learning and developed an online interactive course called *Français interactif*[20] to complement the University of Texas's 'smart' classrooms.

Français interactif is intended for first-year French students. Text is enriched with audio and video clips. The students explore French language and culture by following the lives of real University of Texas students who have been part of the University of Texas Summer Program in Lyon, France. It includes online grammar references with self-correcting exercises and audio dialogues, verb conjugation and practice tools, diagnostic grammar quizzes, a workbook of classroom activities and homework assignments, online polls and Internet writing activities.

The Center is developing online multimedia course material for other languages as well. *Deutsch im Blick*[21] is based on videos of native German speakers and the University of Texas Summer Program in Würzburg, Germany. Like *Français interactif*, it includes audio vocabulary, phonetics lessons, online comparative polls and Internet writing activities. Although these online language curricula were designed to be used at the University of Texas, they are freely available on the web.

Multimedia e-books at the University of Oklahoma

The University of Oklahoma offers several engineering e-textbooks via its eCourses web portal.[22] The textbooks are designed for basic engineering courses and cover Statics, Dynamics, Solid Mechanics, Thermodynamics, Fluids, Maths, MEMS and Multimedia. They can be integrated with the syllabus or used as stand-alones for distance learning.

Users can navigate within the books by clicking on chapters and sections. Each section has a detailed case study of a typical engineering problem, which is used to illustrate the concept covered in that section. There is also a theory page that presents the basic engineering principles and equations needed in the solution. Various media types, such as animations, sounds, graphics and simulations, are used. Each section has a simulation where users can vary the parameters used in the case study. This enables them to better understand what effect each of the variables in the case study has on the solution. The eCourse portal is designed to assist University of Oklahoma students and professors but it is freely available for any person or institution to use. No registration is required.

The material in the e-books was developed by the authors using basic electronic media tools including DreamWeaver (an HTML editor), Flash (a 2D animation and simulation tool), MathType (an equation editor), Carrara (3D animation), PhotoShop (photo editing) and Freehand (a 2D drawing tool). Kurt Gramoll, in his article *A Web-based*

Electronic Book (eBook) for Solid Mechanics, explains that the total cost of these software tools was below $1,000 US, and that, as with any textbook, the main cost was in developing the material. He also says that each module required about 40 hours of development time, including the time to create the graphics.[23]

Laboratórios de Instrumentação para Medição/Laboratories of Instrumentation for Measurement

The bilingual e-book *Laboratórios de Instrumentação para Medição/Laboratories of Instrumentation for Measurement*[24] deals with concepts, methods and procedures related to engineering measurement. It includes hands-on activities, sketches, figures, animations, videos and remote and virtual labs, and integrates many types of multimedia within the written material.

The book has been developed by the engineering faculty of the University of Porto, in Portugal. It is written in Portuguese but it also has an English language version. This allows non-Portuguese-speaking students to use it and also enables Portuguese-speaking users to become familiar with the technical subject terminology in English.

The e-book comprises 13 modules (or chapters). Each of them presents a learning objective, essential concepts and a step-by-step guide to performing an experimental activity, various types of complementary multimedia presentations and a final synthesis. A set of open questions that closes each module is intended to provide formative assessment. Several experiments have also been embedded. All are freely available at the University's Remote Lab.[25] The e-book is in PDF format with Adobe Flash applications embedded in an HTML page.

Undergraduate and postgraduate students who tested the book considered it provided good support in relating information to their own experiences and previous knowledge, and in promoting understanding and long-term retention. The e-book was first used in the 2008/2009 school year. The percentage of students failing has decreased to 0.8 per cent.

E-texts in the classroom

E-books are a part of the wider electronic milieu and as such they have been seen as providing special benefits in the classroom. There are several reasons why they are seen as beneficial, including the increase in academic achievement and the decrease in the cost of student textbooks.

E-books have generally been seen as improving learning outcomes. They can help students to learn more effectively and teachers to become more efficient in their teaching. As new technologies are attractive to many students, using e-books can also be motivating. Various features of e-books can provide support for students with print or reading disabilities. Some e-book programs have interactive dictionaries, providing just-in-time learning, by allowing users to select a word in the e-book and get an instant definition. They can also have the definition read aloud, or request an instant translation to another language. Features such as these can increase students' attention and comprehension.

A number of researchers have looked at the influence of new technologies on student achievement. However, they are not uniformly positive about their role in academic achievement. One example is a study done by Shepperd, Grace and Koch in 2008. They examined the perceptions and performance of nearly 400 students taking an introductory psychology course. They found that the form of the textbook (electronic or paper) did not have any influence on students' grades. They said that students using the e-textbooks reported spending less time on course-related reading but nevertheless evaluated the electronic text unfavourably. No student who purchased an electronic text in a prior class chose to purchase one for the introductory psychology course. The authors suggest that it may be premature to abandon paper texts in favour of electronic ones.[26]

Some researchers argue that it is not the technology itself, but how it is applied. Harold Wenglinsky in his study, *Does it Compute: The Relationship between Educational Technology and Student Achievement in Mathematics*, found that not all uses of technology were beneficial. He argues that using software to create simulations had a positive effect on academic achievement, while using computers to teach low-order thinking skills was counter-productive.[27]

Clark and Mayer also say that it's not delivery mediums, but instructional methods that facilitate learning. Their 2003 study shows that

> when the instructional methods remain essentially the same, so does the learning, no matter how the instruction is delivered. When a course uses effective instructional methods, learning will be better, no matter what delivery medium is used.[28]

However, a number of studies have found that technology does have a positive role in academic achievement. The United States Department of Education conducted a meta-survey of studies that contrasted online and face-to-face learning, from 1996 to July 2008. The meta-study confirmed that higher education students in online learning courses generally performed better than those in face-to-face courses.[29]

Charlotte Johnson and William Harroff argue that e-books can be part of the solution to the illiteracy problem. They point out that

> rather than focusing solely on digitising print text and worrying about redefining the term book, publishers of electronic materials should take full advantage of the multimodal learning styles that can be addressed by well-designed electronic publications.[30]

The cost of student textbooks is a further concern, and authors such as Charles Hannon say that electronic formats will reduce textbook pricing.[31] The amount of money students have to spend on textbooks is significant. In the United States, for example, students spend up to $1,000 per year on textbooks. A study conducted in 2006 by the United States National Association of College Stores has shown that nearly 60 per cent of students choose not to buy all the course materials.[32]

In 2008, the Northwest Missouri State University undertook a study on the feasibility of transitioning from the renting of traditional textbooks to renting e-textbooks. The study involved four faculty members (selection was based mostly on the availability of appropriate e-textbooks for courses). E-textbooks were provided to laptops from several different publisher platforms, including VitalSource and CourseSmart. The survey showed that cost considerations were an important factor in student decision-making with respect to electronic versus print textbooks. When asked if they would prefer electronic over print textbooks if by using electronic the rental would not increase, 55 per cent of the students replied that they would prefer the e-textbooks.[33]

Other findings of this study were that students have a high affinity for handheld electronic devices but that enthusiasm for e-readers quickly wanes in the absence of the desired search and annotation features. Both students and faculty considered keyword searching and annotating as very important features. Students think of e-readers as attention-getters but not attention-keepers. Students also liked the idea of not having to carry heavy textbooks in their backpacks.

The considerations about carrying books have also been raised on the popular blog *TechCrunch*, where Michael Arrington wrote that carrying print books is 'as big a pain as it has been for past generations of students' and that 'a new large screen Kindle would solve those problems'.[34]

In 2009 Princeton University participated in the Amazon Kindle DX pilot program. The majority of students and teachers said they were not pleased with the Kindle's slow performance and limited features and that the Kindle limits interaction with the text. The campus newspaper, *The Daily Princetonian*, published the following comments:

> Much of my learning comes from a physical interaction with the text: bookmarks, highlights, page-tearing, sticky notes and other marks representing the importance of certain passages – not to mention margin notes, where most of my paper ideas come from and interaction with the material occurs. All these things have been lost, and if not lost they're too slow to keep up with my thinking, and the "features" have been rendered useless.[35]

The adoption of e-textbooks is obviously a very complex process, and involves many factors. Kenneth Sherman and Ethel Vesper in their 2009 article, *Monetize Hidden Value in eBooks and Other Digital Learning Assets*, did a meta-study of 14 articles on the applications and benefits of electronic textbooks. The authors conclude that 'transitioning to digital materials impacts not only students, faculty and administrators, but also curriculum development, instructional design, customer service, technical support, academic services and purchasing'. They also say that, to ensure digital transition is completed smoothly, the e-book adoption has to be aligned with the course development process flows and procedures.[36]

In the context of e-textbooks, there has been an interesting initiative by Macmillan, one of the five largest publishers of trade books and textbooks. Macmillan has launched a new software package called *DynamicBooks*.[37] This enables lecturers to customise e-textbooks for their individual classes. Instructors can alter particular sentences and paragraphs without consulting the original authors or publisher, and also upload course syllabuses, notes, videos, pictures and graphs. Because these textbooks are going to be so modifiable, the *New York Times* has called it a kind of 'Wikipedia of textbooks'.[38]

The research literature indicates that, although student and faculty experiences with e-books have been various, they have been mostly positive. As digital technologies continue to transform the environment for teaching, learning and research, we will continue to see new developments with e-books as well.

Notes and references

1. Wilson, R. (2003) 'E-education in the UK', *Journal of Digital Information*, 3(4). Retrieved 4 July 2010 from *http://journals.tdl.org/jodi/article/viewArticle/91/90*.
2. The Sloan Consortium is a consortium of individuals, institutions and organisations committed to quality online education. For more information see *http://www. sloan-c.org*.

3. Allen, I.E. and Seaman, J. (2010) *Learning on Demand: Online Education in the United States, 2009.* Retrieved 4 July 2010 from *http://www.sloanconsortium.org/publications/survey/pdf/learningondemand.pdf.*

4. Paul Budde Communication Pty Ltd (2009) *Global Digital Economy – E-Government, E-Health and E-Education Trends.*

5. Available at *http://ocw.mit.edu* (accessed 4 July 2010).

6. Shiratuddin, N., Landoni, M., Gibb, F. and Hassan, S. (2003) 'E-book technology and its potential applications in distance education', *Journal of Digital Information,* 3(4).

7. Shapiro, J.J. and Hughes, S.K. (1996) 'Information Literacy as a Liberal Art', *Educom Review,* 31(2). Retrieved from *http://net.educause.edu/apps/er/review/reviewArticles/31231.html.*

8. Martin, A. and Rader, H.B. (eds) (2002) *Information and IT Literacy: Enabling Learning in the 21st Century.* London: Facet.

9. CIBER (2008) *Information Behaviour of the Researcher of the Future: a CIBER Briefing Paper.* Available from *http://www.jisc.ac.uk/media/documents/programmes/reppres/gg_final_keynote_11012008.pdf.*

10. Primary Research Group (2009) *The Survey of Higher Education Faculty. Use of Library Reference, Info Literacy and Subject Specialist Staff.* Available from *http://www.library.auckland.ac.nz/eproducts/ebooks/SHEF.pdf.*

11. Schonfeld, R.C. and Housewright, R. (2009) *Faculty Survey 2009: Key Strategic Insights for Libraries, Publishers, and Societies.* Retrieved 4 July 2010 from *http://www.ithaka.org/ithaka-s-r/research/faculty-surveys-2000-2009/Faculty%20Study%202009.pdf.*

12. Schonfeld, R.C. and Guthrie, K.M. (2007) 'The changing information services needs of faculty', *EDUCAUSE*

Review, 42, no. 4 (July/August 2007). Retrieved 4 July 2010 from *http://www.educause.edu/EDUCAUSE+ Review/EDUCAUSEReviewMagazineVolume42/The ChangingInformationServices/161752*.

13. Schonfeld, R.C. and Housewright, R. (2009) *Faculty Survey 2009: Key Strategic Insights for Libraries, Publishers, and Societies.* Retrieved 4 July 2010 from *http://www.ithaka.org/ithaka-s-r/research/faculty-surveys-2000-2009/Faculty%20Study%202009.pdf*.

14. *Oxford Dictionary of English.* (2005) Oxford: Oxford University Press.

15. See *http://en.wikipedia.org/wiki/Book*.

16. Available at *http://web.mit.edu/viz/EM/flash/E&M_ Master/E&M.swf* (accessed 4 July 2010).

17. See *http://web.mit.edu/8.02t/www/802TEAL3D/teal_ tour.htm*.

18. Dori, Y.J. and Belcher, J. (2005) 'Learning electromagnetism with visualizations and active learning', in J. K. Gilbert (ed), *Visualization in Science Education.* Dordrecht: Springer.

19. See *http://tltc.la.utexas.edu/tltc/projects/index.html#dib* (accessed 4 July 2010).

20. Available at *http://www.laits.utexas.edu/fi* (accessed 4 July 2010).

21. Available at *http://tltc.la.utexas.edu/dib/* (accessed 4 July 2010).

22. See *http://www.ecourses.ou.edu/* (accessed 4 July 2010).

23. Gramoll, K. (2007) *A Web-based Electronic Book (eBook) for Solid Mechanics.* Paper presented at the ASEE Annual Conference, Honolulu. Retrieved 6 July 2010 from *http://eml.ou.edu/paper/paper/2007_asee_ fluid_ebook.pdf*.

24. Restivo, M.T., Almeida, F.G., Chouzal, M.d.F., Mendes, J. and Lopes, A.M. (2009) *An Innovative E-book on the*

Measurement Field. Paper presented at the EUNIS International Congress. Retrieved 4 July 2010 from *www.eunis.org/events/congresses/EUNIS2009/p31.pdf.*

25. Available at *http://remotelab.fe.up.pt/* (accessed 4 July 2010).

26. Shepperd, J.A., Grace, J.L. and Koch, E.J. (2008) 'Evaluating the electronic textbook: is it time to dispense with the paper text?' *Teaching of Psychology*, 35(1), 2–5.

27. Wenglinsky, H. (1998) *Does it Compute? The Relationship Between Educational Technology and Student Achievement in Mathematics*. Retrieved 4 July 2010 from *http://www.ets.org/research/policy_research_reports/ pic-technology.*

28. Clark, R.C. and Mayer, R.E. (2003) *E-Learning and the Science of Instruction: Proven Guidelines for Consumers and Designers of Multimedia Learning*, 1st edn. San Francisco, CA: Jossey-Bass/Pfeiffer.

29. Means, B., Toyama, Y., Murphy, R., Bakia, M. and Jones, K. (2009) *Evaluation of Evidence-Based Practices in Online Learning: A Meta-Analysis and Review of Online Learning Studies*. Retrieved 4 July 2010 from *http://www2.ed.gov/rschstat/eval/tech/evidence-based-practices/finalreport.pdf.*

30. Johnson, C. and Harroff, W. (2006) 'The new art of making books', *Library Journal*, 131(7), 8–12.

31. Hannon, C. (2008) 'E-Texts in the classroom: e-text readers designed for use in higher education will reduce textbook pricing and address environmental concerns', *EDUCAUSE Quarterly*, 31(1). Retrieved 4 July 2010 from *http://www.educause.edu/EDUCAUSE+Quarterly /EDUCAUSEQuarterlyMagazineVolum/ETextsinthe Classroom/162511.*

32. Kinzie, S. (23 January 2006). 'Swelling Textbook Costs Have College Students Saying "Pass"', *The*

Washington Post. Retrieved 4 July 2010 from *http://www.washingtonpost.com/wp-dyn/content/article/2006/01/22/AR2006012201290.html*.

33. Rickman, J.T., Holzen, R.V., Klute, P.G. and Tobin, T. (2009) 'A campus-wide e-textbook initiative', *EDUCAUSE Quarterly*, 32(2). Retrieved 4 July 2010 from *http://www.educause.edu/EDUCAUSE+Quarterly/EDUCAUSEQuarterlyMagazineVolum/ACampusWideETextbookInitiative/174581*.

34. Arrington, M. (17 July 2008) 'Amazon to target $5.5 billion textbook market with new Kindle?', *TechCrunch blog*. Retrieved 4 July 2010 from *http://techcrunch.com/2008/07/17/amazon-to-target-55-billion-textbook-market-with-new-kindle/*.

35. Lee, H. (28 September 2009) 'Kindles yet to woo University users', *Daily Princetonian*. Retrieved 4 July 2010 from *http://www.dailyprincetonian.com/2009/09/28/23918/*.

36. Sherman, K.C. and Vesper, E. (2009) *Monetize Hidden Value in eBooks and Other Digital Learning Assets*. Paper presented at the 25th Annual Conference on Distance Teaching & Learning, Madison, WI. Retrieved 4 July 2010 from *http://www.uwex.edu/disted/conference/Resource_library/proceedings/09_20289.pdf*.

37. See *http://dynamicbooks.com/*.

38. Rich, M. (21 February 2010) 'Textbooks that professors can rewrite digitally', *New York Times*. Retrieved 4 July 2010 from *http://www.nytimes.com/2010/02/22/business/media/22textbook.html*.

7

Future considerations

The previous chapters have examined the integration of e-books into academic libraries, administration of e-book collections, and e-book usage in academic libraries. They also covered e-book publishing and e-books as a learning tool. Four issues stand out:

- Barriers to adoption – e-book collections in academic libraries are growing, but their integration into libraries is still not satisfactory.

- E-books in relation to study and research – e-books have the potential to stimulate new forms of book content usage and thus have a great potential for research, study and teaching.

- Lack of relevant content – user studies show that use of scholarly e-books is closely related to the academic year, but lack of relevant content is a big obstacle.

- The opportunities e-books bring to academic libraries – university libraries are a very important provider of e-books, and this opens new possibilities for libraries.

This chapter will discuss these themes in more detail, as they are closely related to the future of e-books in academic libraries.

Barriers to adoption

Academic libraries have recognised the opportunities e-books offer from the beginning. However, e-books have not been integrated into academic library services as well as electronic journals and articles. Obstacles related to the integration of e-books can be grouped around three main problems.

- *Lack of standards* presents numerous challenges for all aspects of collection management – for the acquisition, discovery, and delivery of e-book collections. It prevents e-book management being seamless and streamlined, and creates an environment of confusion and wasted time. Not all e-book formats are compatible with all e-book reading devices. Publishers' and vendors' platforms differ in appearance and navigation and readers find this very confusing. They have to remember how to move from page to page, how to make notes, how to export citations to citation management programs and so on. User studies show that readers in tertiary institutions spend little time in e-books; they dip in and out looking for information. They do not want to waste time remembering how to use e-book features, or on reading user manuals.

  This area is in the hands of publishers, vendors and software and hardware developers.

- *Lack of awareness of e-book collections.* User surveys show that a significant proportion of library users are unaware that their libraries provide any e-books. Libraries need to put more effort into making users aware of their collections but also explain to them how to use them. Due to the lack of standards mentioned above, searching, downloading and reading e-books often require learning new sets of rules and symbols. Academic users have different levels of access to, and experience with technology.

Technology is changing rapidly, and even technically literate people have to spend a large amount of time keeping up with new developments. Libraries should not assume that new generations of students and professors will have that time available.

Libraries should take a more proactive role in this area.

- *Lack of seamless access.* With the ever-increasing amount of information and the proliferation of information sources, simplicity and ease of use of e-book collections is becoming increasingly important. Library catalogues are a popular way of finding e-books, and libraries have started to add MARC records for them. However, this is only a start. Tertiary libraries acquire e-book collections from different publishers, but also other types of electronic and print materials. Various initiatives already under way in this area prove that uniform access to all library material is something users value highly. A single search across all library resources would eliminate the need to consult separate resources and interfaces. Users do not have to jump between multiple systems to search different kinds of materials. However, providing a single search interface brings up a whole range of issues, including Internet availability and reliability of access, availability of adequate software and hardware, metadata quality and Digital Rights Management.

  This area highlights the need for collaboration between e-book vendors and publishers, software developers and libraries.

Librarians cannot fix all the problems related to barriers of adoption, but nevertheless, they should adopt an active role in order to minimise them, so they can maximise the use of e-books. Many barriers can be addressed through careful planning for the integration of e-books into the academic environment. Librarians are not leading the development of the technology, but as information professionals they can influence it with their knowledge of information science and their practical experiences with information management. It is particularly important that librarians adopt an active role in negotiating licences and pricing models that suit the requirements of academic institutions. It is also important that all parties – librarians, e-book providers and publishers – keep talking to each other about these issues, so that the obstacles can be overcome.

E-books in relation to study and research

There is much debate in the literature about which format will prevail – electronic or print. Some authors argue that electronic will replace print, while others do not see electronic as ever being an alternative to print books for all purposes. Most have hedged their bets.

Studies on user behaviour indicate that print and e-books are not used in the same way. In the academic environment, e-books are generally used for quick reference, but for more serious study users prefer print books. Obviously, print books and e-books enable different learning styles, and as Penny Garrod pointed out several years ago, they 'satisfy a different set of needs'.[1]

Both print and electronic formats have their place in academic and research libraries – for the time being at least. Electronic resources tend to complement printed material rather than replace it. With this in mind, libraries should find ways to offer both options to their users.

Electronic text has functionalities that print cannot offer, including hyperlinking, text-to-speech functionality and possibilities of being 'illustrated' by multimedia. Most studies show that electronic textbooks have a positive effect on learning outcomes. E-books have an especially important role in distance, mobile and e-learning, and the continuous growth of electronic classroom learning is expected to highlight the need for more of them.

Another issue puzzling many commentators is why e-journals so quickly found a dominant place in academia while e-books lagged behind. The 2009 Ithaka S+R survey found that faculty considered e-journals were very important for their research and teaching. At the same time, e-books were identified as least important.[2] However, the survey done by Satisfaction Management Systems (SMS) and Elsevier's Science & Technology Division shows that researchers value e-books, and that, in most stages of their research, books are more important than journals (Figure 7.1).[3]

Figure 7.1 Value of books and journals to researchers depending on the stages of the research workflow

Researchers rate the value of content at each stage of the research workflow

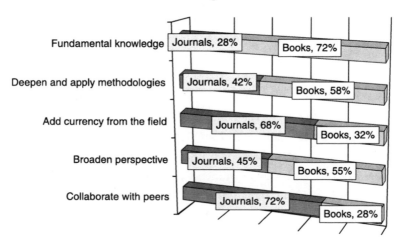

The general opinion is that the successful integration of e-journals is a result of publishers and vendors working closely with libraries in developing business models that are satisfactory for all.

E-journal articles very much imitate print articles in the sense that they do not have many of the extra functionalities that electronic text allows. On the other hand, e-books have often been praised for having these very functionalities. However, most of the e-book collections provided by vendors and publishers are also only an electronic version of a print book. The critical difference is that one can download and print whole articles from journals, whereas many e-book platforms restrict users to a few pages at the time. The rules relating to sharing resources via interlibrary lending are also different for book and journal collections. Electronic e-articles fulfil users' needs for quick access and reading, while e-books are seen as a kind of text that can enhance learning by using the extra functionalities of electronic text. Further research would clarify these issues.

A number of studies on e-books argue that e-books offer new way of approaching text. The Springer study, *Ebooks – The End User Perspective*, says:

> Overall, the survey results indicate that eBooks are best suited for research purposes or in a search environment where the user needs to locate specific information. Users are not reading eBooks cover-to-cover in the traditional sense but instead approach them as a resource for finding answers to research questions. eBooks have the potential to stimulate new forms of book content usage and will require libraries to think differently about how to accommodate the needs of users as their eBook collections grow.[4]

David Nicholas, head of University College London Information Studies, argues that librarians are still too preoccupied with resources and content and are

> still trotting out the 'fact' that content is king; when in fact the consumer is very much the king now, and we need to know what the king (consumer) is up to.[5]

In this context, a very interesting study on how students search and retrieve information from electronic texts was done by Susan Wilkinson. She observed eye movements as students looked at online material, and in her article, *Maximising student learning through minimising information search time; the role of satisficing and skimming*, she says that students integrate the process of quality judgement with their learning.

> Students are very specific in their behaviour when searching for information from on-line texts. They will not waste time judging the texts/sources before choosing one to study, and they will not judge an entire text/ source on the basis of its first page/paragraph, without skim-checking the remainder before leaving. This has led to a nested model of adaptive time allocation called the 'satisfice then skim-check strategy', whereby students use paragraphs/sections as a patch with which they can satisfice, but then skim-check the remainder of the paragraphs/sections on the page before moving to the next page. This model explains the search strategies used by students when learning from on-line texts, and has implications for the way in which on-line education environments should be designed.[6]

More studies in this field would shed more light on user preferences and help publishers design texts to facilitate learning processes and improve learning outcomes.

Lack of relevant content

Both user surveys and statistics on the usage of library e-book collections show that student reading is closely related to the academic year. Usage peaks when assignments are due and titles prescribed as recommended reading get accessed hundreds of times during these weeks. This means that if we want students to use e-books, they have to be related to courses.

The importance of content and its relation to e-book adoption in academic libraries was highlighted in the 2010 Horizon report. The report concludes that:

> Campuses have been slower to adopt electronic books than the general public for three primary reasons, but all of them are becoming less of a constraint. The primary obstacle was simply availability. While a great variety of consumer titles are available electronically, textbooks or academic works have been published in electronic formats far less frequently. Secondly, as the reader technology developed, the ability to easily render high quality illustrations was initially limited. The last obstacle was related to the publishing model. Where electronic versions were available, they were most commonly viewed as ancillary to the printed version, which had to be purchased before the electronic version could be accessed – and the early versions were not in formats compatible with most readers. Over the past year or so, however, those obstacles have each started to fall away.[7]

Provision of electronic textbooks seems to be a point of major concern for publishers. Although they are generally keen to satisfy library demand for electronic textbooks, publishers worry that allowing textbooks to be published in electronic format will have a catastrophic effect on their print sales. Surprisingly, a JISC (Joint Information Systems Committee) study suggests that provision of electronic course texts does not impact on print sales.[8] The study involved 36 core textbooks supplied free-at-the-point-of-use to teachers and students at 127 universities in the United Kingdom from November 2007 to December 2008. Print sales of these 36 textbooks did not decline over this period. JISC acknowledges that the sample was small in size, and as such, it does not really allow for generalisation.

UK publisher Palgrave Macmillan's managing director Dominic Knight has been reported as arguing that the report's findings cannot be relied on, because of the size of the sample. He says:

> The key issue is that textbooks are bought by many millions of students. If the JISC model is to buy a single book to network to students, then the library will have to pay quite a lot.[9]

The demand for e-textbooks within higher education institutions is significant. Universities are concerned with both the price of print textbooks and the lack of electronic textbooks. The need for further studies in this field has been recognised and several projects are under the way. The University of Cincinnati and OhioLINK[10] are working with publishers and university bookstores to provide students with the alternative of purchasing print or electronic textbooks.[11] JISC too have undertaken additional studies on the economic impact of e-textbook business models on publishers, e-book aggregators and universities, including a trial of business models for library-mediated access to e-textbooks. The final report was scheduled to appear in August 2010.[12]

E-books will only be widely used in the academic environment if they fulfil the primary role of support for teaching and learning. For this to happen, libraries need more relevant titles and content. Without it e-book collections will remain marginal. The lack of sustainable business models has been seen as the key barrier to enabling libraries to provide electronic textbooks to the degree that they would like. The JISC recommendation that publishers should develop better platforms for electronic texts, that they should remove some of the digital rights management restrictions and make content available to plagiarism detection software vendors,[13] sounds like a good solution to this problem from the point of view of libraries.

The opportunities e-books bring to academic libraries

It is frequently said that e-books open up new possibilities for academic libraries. Connaway and Wicht, in their 2007 article, 'What happened to the e-book revolution?' write:

> Although there are still barriers to the adoption of e-books in academic libraries, e-books provide an opportunity for librarians to offer the academic community what they want – direct access to full-text content.[14]

Similarly, the Springer survey emphasises that e-books offer academic libraries 'important opportunities for enhancing the user research experience'.[15]

Any time, any place access to full text material is the goal of today's virtual scholar. The most important characteristics associated with e-book content are accessibility, flexibility, searchability and convenience.

Libraries should take the opportunity to strengthen ties with their users. Libraries have been a very important source of scholarly e-books. Students and faculty increasingly rely on collections provided via their libraries. But studies also show that the demand for e-books has been outrunning the supply. In the SMS and Elsevier study a significant number of researchers indicated that they would like to access and use online books but do not have access through their libraries.[16] Libraries that are still hesitant to provide electronic books should acquire at least a few collections as a start.

The future of e-books in academic libraries

The future will be shaped by a number of factors.

Changes in the area of e-book technology are constant and reflect the increasing popularity of e-books. The development of wireless broadband networks, more affordable and lighter e-book readers and better screen displays have made the general public more comfortable with reading content from computer screens and mobile telephones, and they are increasingly purchasing electronic books. New generations of students will come to the universities with new sets of expectations.

Another important driver of change is the speed and direction of technological developments in the field of teaching and learning. New hybrid and interactive media types are already emerging. Particularly important are developments related to distance, mobile and e-learning. The increasing need for more electronic texts in these areas is obvious, and libraries must be able to support these media types.

The shift towards electronic formats by the academic community is well advanced. It is difficult to say when, or if, electronic will totally replace print, but the trend will not reverse. Library collections will include even more electronic material in years to come.

The question is not *if*, but *how* to provide e-books so that they can be used to their maximum potential. Libraries have an important role in making that happen.

Notes and references

1. Garrod, P. (2004) 'E-books: are they the interlibrary lending model of the future?', *Interlending & Document Supply*, 32(4), 227–233. Retrieved 4 July 2010 from *www.emeraldinsight.com/10.1108/02641610410567971*.
2. Schonfeld, R.C. and Housewright, R. (2009) *Faculty Survey 2009: Key Strategic Insights for Libraries, Publishers, and Societies*. Retrieved 4 July 2010 from *http://www.ithaka.org/ithaka-s-r/research/faculty-surveys-2000-2009/Faculty%20Study%202009.pdf*.
3. Herbst, T. (2009) 'What is the value of content to the research workflow? A recent study found that online access to eBooks is key', *Library Connect*, 7(3). Retrieved 4 July 2010 from *http://libraryconnect.elsevier.com/lcn/0703/lcn070310.html*.
4. *eBooks – The End User Perspective* (2008) Retrieved 4 July 2010 from *http://www.springer.com/cda/content/document/cda_downloaddocument/eBooks+-+the+End+User+Experience?SGWID=0-0-45-608298-0*.
5. Nicholas, D. (2008) 'The information-seeking behaviour of the virtual scholar: from use to users', *Serials: The Journal for the Serials Community*, 21(2). Available from

http://uksg.metapress.com/media/4g117bnyxr2rrkbpty47/ contributions/h/0/0/7/h007v25j5587437h.pdf.

6. Wilkinson, S. (2010) 'Maximising student learning through minimising information search time; the role of satisficing and skimming', *Journal of Learning Development in Higher Education*, 2 (February). Retrieved 4 July 2010 from *http://www.aldinhe.ac.uk/ ojs/index.php?journal=jldhe&page=issue&op=view&p ath%5B%5D=9.*

7. Johnson, L., Levine, A., Smith, R. and Stone, S. (2010) *The 2010 Horizon Report.* Retrieved 4 July 2010 from *http://www.educause.edu/ELI/2010HorizonReport/ 195400.*

8. JISC (2009) *Assessing the impact of electronic course texts on print sales and library hard copy circulation: CIBER, Final Report, November 2009.* Retrieved 4 July 2010 from *http://www.ucl.ac.uk/infostudies/ research/ciber/printsales.pdf.*

9. Bury, L. (17 September 2009) 'Publisher cautious over positive e-book study', *The Bookseller.com.* Retrieved 4 July 2010 from *http://www.thebookseller.com/news/ 97234-publisher-cautious-over-positive-e-book-study. html.*

10. See *http://ohdbks.lib.overdrive.com/F73EC46C-D0F2- 45AF-AA50-B2DC7E1D5B19/10/364/en/Libraries. htm* (accessed 4 July 2010).

11. Schaffhauser, D. (22 April 2010) 'U Cincinnati and OhioLINK Research Digital Textbook Adoption', Retrieved 4 July 2010 from *http://campustechnology. comArticles/2010/04/22/U-Cincinnati-and-Ohio LINK-Research-Digital-Textbook-Adoption.aspx.*

12. See *http://www.jiscebooksproject.org/business-models* (accessed 4 July 2010).

13. JISC (2009) *Assessing the impact of electronic course texts on print sales and library hard copy circulation: CIBER, Final Report, November 2009.* Retrieved 4 July 2010 from *http://www.ucl.ac.uk/infostudies/research/ciber/printsales.pdf.*

14. Connaway, C.L. and Wicht, H.L. (2007) 'What happened to the e-book revolution?', *Journal of Electronic Publishing,* 10(3).

15. *eBooks – The End User Perspective* (2008) Retrieved 4 July 2010 from *http://www.springer.com/cda/content/document/cda_downloaddocument/eBooks+-+the+End+User+Experience?SGWID=0-0-45-608298-0.*

16. Herbst, T. (2009) 'What is the value of content to the research workflow? A recent study found that online access to eBooks is key', *Library Connect,* 7(3). Retrieved 4 July 2010 from *http://libraryconnect.elsevier.com/lcn/0703/lcn070310.html.*

Index

Breinigsville, PA USA
11 January 2011
253139BV00004B/1/P